VITAL
IDEAS
MONEY

Other books in the VITAL IDEAS series:

VITAL IDEAS: Crime
Edited by Theresa Starkey

VITAL IDEAS: Sex
Edited by Regina Barreca

VITAL IDEAS: Work
Edited by Christina Boufis

Series Editor: Daniel Born, academic department chair in Kaplan University's legal studies department and lecturer in the MA literature program at Northwestern University's School of Continuing Studies

Volume Editors: Dana Heller, professor and chair of English at Old Dominion University; Claire Pamplin, assistant professor of English at the Borough of Manhattan Community College of the City University of New York

Contributors
Kristine Bergman
Nancy Carr
Steven Craig
Patrick Hurley
Mary Klein
Dylan Nelson
Amy Schuler
Donald H. Whitfield
Mary Williams

VITAL
IDEAS
MONEY

Edited by Dana Heller
and
Claire Pamplin

THE GREAT BOOKS FOUNDATION
A nonprofit educational organization

Published and distributed by

THE GREAT BOOKS FOUNDATION

A nonprofit educational organization

35 E. Wacker Drive, Suite 400
Chicago, Illinois 60601
www.greatbooks.org

First printing
9 8 7 6 5 4 3 2 1

Library of Congress Cataloging-in-Publication Data

Vital ideas : money / edited by Dana Heller and Claire Pamplin.
    p. cm.
 ISBN 978-1-933147-80-2 (alk. paper)
 1. Money. 2. Inquiry-based learning. I. Heller, Dana A.
(Dana Alice), 1959- II. Pamplin, Claire. III. Title: Money.
 HG221.3.V58 2011
 332.4--dc23

                              2011028114

Book cover and interior design: THINK Book Works

About the
Great Books Foundation

The Great Books Foundation, publisher of the Vital Ideas series, was established in 1947 by University of Chicago educators Robert Maynard Hutchins and Mortimer Adler. The Foundation is an independent, nonprofit educational organization whose mission is to empower readers of all ages to become more reflective and responsible thinkers. To this end, the Foundation publishes enduring works across the disciplines and conducts workshops in Shared Inquiry,™ a text-based, Socratic method of learning.

Footnotes by an author are not bracketed; footnotes by the Great Books Foundation, an editor, or a translator are [bracketed].

Spelling and punctuation have been modernized and slightly altered for clarity.

Contents

Preface

Money as a medium of exchange has been around since civilization evolved beyond the barter system. Whether we possess large sums of it or crave more of it, thinking about it can keep us awake at night. It is the stuff of obsessive dreams, and of the American dream. It has been reviled by saints, sages, and social theorists, but it is also universally understood as the means of keeping modern society functioning and afloat. How are we to consider this thing that sometimes seems a simultaneous blessing and curse? In this Vital Ideas volume we consider, among others, the voices of African American women, a leading Transcendentalist thinker who tries to live simply, and an urban anthropologist who studies the way the modern shopping mall markets women's underwear. Listening to them, we just might start making sense out of that complicated concept we call money.

The Vital Ideas series takes a content-based rather than skills-based approach to reading and composition. It is based on the conviction, supported by the editors' own classroom experience, that students are most motivated to improve their reading and writing skills when they are engaged with subject matter that is meaningful to them. The contents of each volume represent outstanding examples of well-reasoned thought and high-quality writing across a variety of genres. In keeping with the tradition of the Great Books Foundation, the Vital Ideas series is first and foremost designed to stimulate rewarding Shared Inquiry discussions and instill the habits of reflective, critical thinking.

Using the Questions

Each of the selections in this volume is followed by two sets of questions that will help enrich the reader's engagement with what the author has to say.

The "For Discussion" questions ask about the meaning of what the author says, often referring to a specific phrase or passage in the selection. These questions ask readers to form interpretations of the text and are particularly helpful for initiating classroom discussion. They are closely connected with the practice of Shared Inquiry discussion, described at the back of this volume in the "About Shared Inquiry" section.

The questions designated "For Further Reflection" generally ask for a broader response to the selection. These questions work well in conjunction with the "For Discussion" questions but can also be used as prompts for writing assignments, since they encourage not only interpretations of the text, but also the evaluation of its ideas.

In addition, at the back of the book is a set of "Comparison Questions." These questions encourage discussion and writing about issues that are common to tw o or more selections in the book. Unlike the generic "compare and contrast" questions in many textbooks, the "Comparison Questions" ask readers to critically address specific ideas and points of view that the authors have expressed.

Harriet Jacobs (1813–1897) was born a slave and grew up in Edenton, North Carolina. After refusing to become her owner's mistress, she was sent to his son's plantation. Jacobs had two children with Samuel Tredwell Sawyer, a white lawyer who lived nearby. The children lived with Jacobs's grandmother, a freed slave. When it appeared that they would be moved to the plantation to be raised as slaves, Jacobs faked her escape, knowing this would force their sale. They were purchased by their father and later sent North to freedom. After seven years in hiding, Jacobs escaped to New York City. She later moved to Rochester, where she worked in the abolition movement. In 1853 she began writing *Incidents in the Life of a Slave Girl*, from which this selection is taken. She self-published her book in 1861. It is one of the most widely read examples of the "slave narrative," a mainstay of early African American literature.

The New Master and Mistress

Dr. Flint, a physician in the neighborhood, had married the sister of my mistress, and I was now the property of their little daughter. It was not without murmuring that I prepared for my new home, and what added to my unhappiness was the fact that my brother William was purchased by the same family. My father, by his nature as well as by the habit of transacting business as a skillful mechanic, had more of the feelings of a freeman than is common among slaves. My brother was a spirited boy, and being brought up under such influences he early detested the name of master and mistress. One day, when his father and his mistress both happened to call him at the same time, he hesitated between the two, being perplexed to know which had the strongest claim upon his obedience. He finally concluded to go to his mistress. When my father reproved him for it he said, "You both called me, and I didn't know which I ought to go to first."

"You are *my* child," replied our father, "and when I call you, you should come immediately, if you have to pass through fire and water."

Poor Willie! He was now to learn his first lesson of obedience to a master. Grandmother tried to cheer us with hopeful words, and they found an echo in the credulous hearts of youth.

When we entered our new home we encountered cold looks, cold words, and cold treatment. We were glad when the night came. On my narrow bed I moaned and wept; I felt so desolate and alone.

I had been there nearly a year when a dear little friend of mine was buried. I heard her mother sob as the clods fell on the coffin of her only child, and I turned away from the grave, feeling thankful that I still had something left to love. I met my grandmother, who said, "Come with me, Linda," and from her tone I knew that something sad had happened.[1] She led me apart from the people, and then said, "My child, your father is dead." Dead! How could I believe it? He had died so suddenly I had not even heard that he was sick. I went home with my grandmother. My heart rebelled against God, who had taken from me mother, father, mistress, and friend. The good grandmother tried to comfort me. "Who knows the ways of God?" said she. "Perhaps they have been kindly taken from the evil days to come." Years afterwards I often thought of this. She promised to be a mother to her grandchildren, so far as she might be permitted to do so, and strengthened by her love I returned to my master's. I thought I should be allowed to go to my father's house the next morning, but I was ordered to go for flowers, that my mistress's house might be decorated for an evening party. I spent the day gathering flowers and weaving them into festoons, while the dead body of my father was lying within a mile of me. What cared my owners for that? He was merely a piece of property. Moreover, they thought he had spoiled his children by teaching them to feel that they were human beings. This was blasphemous doctrine for a slave to teach, presumptuous in him and dangerous to the masters.

---

1. [Harriet Jacobs used the name "Linda Brent" to conceal her identity as the subject and author of her story.]

The next day I followed his remains to a humble grave beside that of my dear mother. There were those who knew my father's worth and respected his memory.

My home now seemed more dreary than ever. The laugh of the little slave children sounded harsh and cruel. It was selfish to feel so about the joy of others. My brother moved about with a very grave face. I tried to comfort him by saying, "Take courage, Willie; brighter days will come by and by."

"You don't know anything about it, Linda," he replied. "We shall have to stay here all our days; we shall never be free."

I argued that we were growing older and stronger, and that perhaps we might, before long, be allowed to hire our own time, and then we could earn money to buy our freedom. William declared this was much easier to say than to do; moreover, he did not intend to *buy* his freedom. We held daily controversies upon this subject.

Little attention was paid to the slaves' meals in Dr. Flint's house. If they could catch a bit of food while it was going, well and good. I gave myself no trouble on that score, for on my various errands I passed my grandmother's house, where there was always something to spare for me. I was frequently threatened with punishment if I stopped there, and my grandmother, to avoid detaining me, often stood at the gate with something for my breakfast or dinner. I was indebted to *her* for all my comforts, spiritual or temporal. It was *her* labor that supplied my scanty wardrobe. I have a vivid recollection of the linsey-woolsey dress given me every winter by Mrs. Flint. How I hated it! It was one of the badges of slavery.

While my grandmother was thus helping to support me from her hard earnings, the three hundred dollars she had lent her mistress were never repaid. When her mistress died, her son–in–law, Dr. Flint, was appointed executor. When grandmother applied to him for payment, he said the estate was insolvent and the law prohibited payment. It did not, however, prohibit him from retaining the silver candelabra, which had been purchased with that money. I presume they will be handed down in the family, from generation to generation.

My grandmother's mistress had always promised her that, at her death, she should be free, and it was said that in her will she made good the promise. But when the estate was settled, Dr. Flint told the faithful old servant that, under existing circumstances, it was necessary she should be sold.

On the appointed day, the customary advertisement was posted up, proclaiming that there would be a "public sale of Negroes, horses, &c." Dr. Flint called to tell my grandmother that he was unwilling to wound her feelings by putting her up at auction, and that he would prefer to dispose of her at private sale. My grandmother saw through his hypocrisy; she understood very well that he was ashamed of the job. She was a very spirited woman, and if he was base enough to sell her when her mistress intended she should be free, she was determined the public should know it. She had for a long time supplied many families with crackers and preserves; consequently, "Aunt Marthy," as she was called, was generally known, and everybody who knew her respected her intelligence and good character. Her long and faithful service in the family was also well known, and the intention of her mistress to leave her free. When the day of sale came, she took her place among the chattels, and at the first call she sprang upon the auction block. Many voices called out, "Shame! Shame! Who is going to sell *you*, Aunt Marthy? Don't stand there! That is no place for *you*." Without saying a word, she quietly awaited her fate. No one bid for her. At last, a feeble voice said, "Fifty dollars." It came from a maiden lady, seventy years old, the sister of my grandmother's deceased mistress. She had lived forty years under the same roof with my grandmother; she knew how faithfully she had served her owners and how cruelly she had been defrauded of her rights, and she resolved to protect her. The auctioneer waited for a higher bid but her wishes were respected; no one bid above her. She could neither read nor write, and when the bill of sale was made out, she signed it with a cross. But what consequence was that, when she had a big heart overflowing with human kindness? She gave the old servant her freedom.

At that time, my grandmother was just fifty years old. Laborious years had passed since then, and now my brother and I were slaves to the man who had defrauded her of her money and tried to defraud her of her freedom. One of my mother's sisters, called Aunt Nancy, was also a slave in his family. She was a kind, good aunt to me, and supplied the place of both housekeeper and waiting maid to her mistress. She was, in fact, at the beginning and end of everything.

Mrs. Flint, like many Southern women, was totally deficient in energy. She had not strength to superintend her household affairs, but her nerves were so strong that she could sit in her easy chair and see a woman whipped till the blood trickled from every stroke of the lash. She was a member of the church, but partaking of the Lord's supper did not seem to put her in a Christian frame of mind. If dinner was not served at the exact time on that particular Sunday, she would station herself in the kitchen and wait till it was dished and then spit in all the kettles and pans that had been used for cooking. She did this to prevent the cook and her children from eking out their meager fare with the remains of the gravy and other scrapings. The slaves could get nothing to eat except what she chose to give them. Provisions were weighed out by the pound and ounce, three times a day. I can assure you she gave them no chance to eat wheat bread from her flour barrel. She knew how many biscuits a quart of flour would make and exactly what size they ought to be.

Dr. Flint was an epicure. The cook never sent a dinner to his table without fear and trembling; for if there happened to be a dish not to his liking, he would either order her to be whipped or compel her to eat every mouthful of it in his presence. The poor, hungry creature might not have objected to eating it, but she did object to having her master cram it down her throat till she choked.

They had a pet dog that was a nuisance in the house. The cook was ordered to make some Indian mush for him. He refused to eat, and when his head was held over it, the froth flowed from his mouth into the basin. He died a few minutes after. When Dr. Flint came in, he said the mush had not been well cooked and that was the reason the animal would not eat it. He sent for the cook and compelled her to eat it. He thought that the woman's stomach was stronger than the dog's, but her sufferings afterwards proved that he was mistaken. This poor woman endured many cruelties from her master and mistress; sometimes she was locked up, away from her nursing baby, for a whole day and night.

When I had been in the family a few weeks, one of the plantation slaves was brought to town by order of his master. It was near night when he arrived, and Dr. Flint ordered him to be taken to the workhouse and tied up to the joist so that his feet would just escape the ground. In that situation he was to wait till the doctor had taken his tea. I shall never forget that night. Never before in my life had I heard hundreds of blows fall, in succession, on a human being. His piteous groans and his "O, pray don't, massa," rang in my ear for months afterwards. There were many conjectures as to the cause of this terrible punishment. Some said master accused him of stealing corn; others said the slave had quarrelled with his wife in presence of the overseer and had accused his master of being the father of her child. They were both black, and the child was very fair.

I went into the workhouse next morning, and saw the cowhide still wet with blood and the boards all covered with gore. The poor man lived and continued to quarrel with his wife. A few months afterwards Dr. Flint handed them both over to a slave trader. The guilty man put their value into his pocket and had the satisfaction of knowing that they were out of sight and hearing. When the mother was delivered into the trader's hands, she said, "You *promised* to treat me well." To which he replied, "You have let your tongue run too far, damn you!" She had forgotten that it was a crime for a slave to tell who was the father of her child.

From others than the master, persecution also comes in such cases. I once saw a young slave girl dying soon after the birth of a child nearly white. In her agony she cried out, "O Lord, come and take me!" Her mistress stood by and mocked at her like an incarnate fiend. "You suffer, do you?" she exclaimed. "I am glad of it. You deserve it all, and more too."

The girl's mother said, "The baby is dead, thank God, and I hope my poor child will soon be in heaven, too."

"Heaven!" retorted the mistress. "There is no such place for the like of her and her bastard."

The poor mother turned away, sobbing. Her dying daughter called her, feebly, and as she bent over her,

11

I heard her say, " Don't grieve so, mother; God knows all about it and He will have mercy upon me."

Her sufferings, afterwards, became so intense that her mistress felt unable to stay, but when she left the room, the scornful smile was still on her lips. Seven children called her mother. The poor black woman had but the one child, whose eyes she saw closing in death, while she thanked God for taking her away from the greater bitterness of life.

FOR DISCUSSION

1. Why do the slave owners think that Jacobs's father spoiled his children by teaching them "to feel that they were human beings"? (6)

2. Why do people at the slave auction protest when Harriet's grandmother, "Aunt Marthy," is offered for sale? Why is the low bid of the woman who grew up with Aunt Marthy respected, and the woman allowed to buy Aunt Marthy and free her?

3. Why does Jacobs describe in such detail the cruelty of the Flints toward their slaves?

4. How does the Flints' behavior toward their slaves illustrate their view of slaves as property?

FOR FURTHER REFLECTION

1. How were many slave owners able to justify to themselves their brutal treatment of slaves?

2. If you were the author's father, how would you teach your children that they are human beings, given the constantly dehumanizing conditions of slavery?

Henry David Thoreau (1817–1862) was an American essayist, poet, philosopher, and abolitionist. He was born in Concord, Massachusetts, and attended Harvard University. Greatly influenced by his friend, mentor, and neighbor Ralph Waldo Emerson, as well as the emerging transcendentalist movement, Thoreau began writing poems and essays shortly after graduation. In 1845 Thoreau built a small cabin on land owned by Emerson near Concord. There he wrote *Walden* (1854), from which this selection is taken. In *Walden* Thoreau pays homage to many of the core principles of transcendentalism, celebrating individualism, the inquisitive mind, and the world's natural wonders. Thoreau later became involved in the abolition movement and wrote his important essay, "Civil Disobedience" (1849). Thoreau established a tradition of nature writing and is sometimes called the father of environmentalism.

Economy
(selection)

I see young men, my townsmen, whose misfortune it is to have inherited farms, houses, barns, cattle, and farming tools; for these are more easily acquired than got rid of. Better if they had been born in the open pasture and suckled by a wolf, that they might have seen with clearer eyes what field they were called to labor in. Who made them serfs of the soil? Why should they eat their sixty acres, when man is condemned to eat only his peck of dirt? Why should they begin digging their graves as soon as they are born? They have got to live a man's life, pushing all these things before them, and get on as well as they can. How many a poor immortal soul have I met well nigh crushed and smothered under its load, creeping down the road of life, pushing before it a barn seventy-five feet by forty, its Augean stables never cleansed, and one hundred acres of land, tillage, mowing, pasture, and wood lot! The portionless, who struggle with no such unnecessary inherited encumbrances, find it labor enough to subdue and cultivate a few cubic feet of flesh.

But men labor under a mistake. The better part of the man is soon ploughed into the soil for compost. By a seeming fate, commonly called necessity, they are employed, as it says in an old book, laying up treasures which moth and rust will corrupt and thieves break through and steal. It is a fool's life, as they will find when they get to the end of it, if not before. It is said that Deucalion and Pyrrha created men by throwing stones over their heads behind them:

Inde genus durum sumus, experiensque laborum,
Et documenta damus quâ simus origine nati.

Or, as Raleigh rhymes it in his sonorous way,

From thence our kind hard-hearted is, enduring
    pain and care,
Approving that our bodies of a stony nature are.

So much for a blind obedience to a blundering oracle, throwing the stones over their heads behind them, and not seeing where they fell.

Most men, even in this comparatively free country, through mere ignorance and mistake, are so occupied with the factitious cares and superfluously coarse labors of life that its finer fruits cannot be plucked by them. Their fingers, from excessive toil, are too clumsy and tremble too much for that. Actually, the laboring man has not leisure for a true integrity day by day; he cannot afford to sustain the manliest relations to men; his labor would be depreciated in the market. He has no time to be anything but a machine. How can he remember well his ignorance—which his growth requires—who has so often to use his knowledge? We should feed and clothe him gratuitously sometimes, and recruit him with our cordials, before we judge of him. The finest qualities of our nature, like the bloom on fruits, can be preserved only by the most delicate handling. Yet we do not treat ourselves nor one another thus tenderly.

Some of you, we all know, are poor, find it hard to live, are sometimes, as it were, gasping for breath. I have no doubt that some of you who read this book are unable to pay for all the dinners which you have actually eaten, or for the coats and shoes which are fast wearing or are already worn out, and have come to this page to spend borrowed or stolen time, robbing your creditors of an hour. It is very evident what mean and sneaking lives many of you live, for my sight has been whetted by experience; always on the limits, trying to get into business and trying to get out of debt, a very ancient slough, called by the Latins *aes alienum*, another's brass, for some of their coins were made of brass; still living, and dying, and buried by this other's brass; always promising to pay, promising to pay, tomorrow, and dying today, insolvent; seeking to curry favor, to get custom, by how many modes, only not state-prison offenses; lying, flattering, voting, contracting yourselves into a nutshell of civility, or dilating into an atmosphere of thin and vaporous generosity, that you may persuade your neighbor to let you make his shoes, or his hat, or his coat, or his carriage, or import his groceries for him; making yourselves sick, that you may lay up something against a sick day, something to be tucked away in an old chest, or in a stocking behind the plastering, or, more safely, in the brick bank; no matter where, no matter how much or how little.

I sometimes wonder that we can be so frivolous, I may almost say, as to attend to the gross but somewhat foreign form of servitude called Negro Slavery, there are so many keen and subtle masters that enslave both North and South. It is hard to have a Southern overseer; it is worse to have a Northern one; but worst of all when you are the slave driver of yourself. Talk of a divinity in man! Look at the teamster on the highway, wending to market by day or night; does any divinity stir within him? His highest duty to fodder and water his horses! What is his destiny to him compared with the shipping interests? Does not he drive for Squire Make-a-stir? How godlike, how immortal, is he? See how he cowers and sneaks, how vaguely all the day he fears, not being immortal nor divine, but the slave and prisoner of his own opinion of himself, a fame won by his own deeds. Public opinion is a weak tyrant compared with our own private opinion. What a man thinks of himself, that it is which determines, or rather indicates, his fate. Self-emancipation even in the West Indian provinces of the fancy and imagination—what Wilberforce is there to bring that about? Think, also, of the ladies of the land weaving toilet cushions against the last day, not to betray too green an interest in their fates! As if you could kill time without injuring eternity.

The mass of men lead lives of quiet desperation. What is called resignation is confirmed desperation. From the desperate city you go into the desperate country, and have to console yourself with the bravery of minks and muskrats. A stereotyped but unconscious despair is concealed even under what are called the games and amusements of mankind. There is no play in them, for this comes after work. But it is a characteristic of wisdom not to do desperate things.

When we consider what, to use the words of the catechism, is the chief end of man, and what are the true necessaries and means of life, it appears as if men had desperately chosen the common mode of living because they preferred it to any other. Yet they honestly think there is no choice left. But alert and healthy natures remember that the sun rose clear. It is never too late to give up our prejudices. No way of thinking or doing, however ancient, can be trusted without proof. What everybody echoes or in silence passes by as true today may turn out to be falsehood tomorrow, mere smoke of opinion, which some had trusted for a cloud that would sprinkle fertilizing rain on their fields. What old people say you cannot do you try and find that you can. Old deeds for old people, and new deeds for new. Old people did not know enough once, perchance, to fetch fresh fuel to keep the fire a-going; new people put a little dry wood under a pot, and are whirled round the globe with the speed of birds, in a way to kill old people, as the phrase is. Age is no better, hardly so well, qualified for an instructor as youth, for it has not profited so much as it has lost. One may almost doubt if the wisest man has learned anything of absolute value by living. Practically, the old have no very important advice to give the young, their own experience has been so partial, and their lives have been such miserable failures, for private reasons, as they must believe; and it may be that they have some faith left which belies that experience, and they are only less young than they were. I have lived some thirty years on this planet, and I have yet to hear the first syllable of valuable or even earnest advice from my seniors. They have told me nothing, and probably cannot tell me anything to the purpose. Here is life, an experiment to a great extent untried by me; but it does not avail me that they have tried it. If I have any experience which I think valuable, I am sure to reflect that this my Mentors said nothing about.

One farmer says to me, "You cannot live on vegetable food solely, for it furnishes nothing to make bones with"; and so he religiously devotes a part of his day to supplying his system with the raw material of bones; walking all the while he talks behind his oxen, which, with vegetable-made bones, jerk him and his lumbering plough along in spite of every obstacle. Some things are really necessaries of life in some circles, the most helpless and diseased, which in others are luxuries merely, and in others still are entirely unknown.

The whole ground of human life seems to some to have been gone over by their predecessors, both the heights and the valleys, and all things to have been cared for. According to Evelyn, "the wise Solomon prescribed ordinances for the very distances of trees; and the Roman praetors have decided how often you may go into your neighbor's land to gather the acorns which fall on it without trespass, and what share belongs to that neighbor." Hippocrates has even left directions how we should cut our nails; that is, even with the ends of the fingers, neither shorter nor longer. Undoubtedly the very tedium and ennui which presume to have exhausted the variety and the joys of life are as old as Adam. But man's capacities have never been measured; nor are we to judge of what he can do by any precedents, so little has been tried. Whatever have been thy failures hitherto, "be not afflicted, my child, for who shall assign to thee what thou hast left undone?"

We might try our lives by a thousand simple tests; as, for instance, that the same sun which ripens my beans illuminates at once a system of earths like ours. If I had remembered this it would have prevented some mistakes. This was not the light in which I hoed them. The stars are the apexes of what wonderful triangles! What distant and different beings in the various mansions of the universe are contemplating the same one at the same moment! Nature and human life are as various as our several constitutions. Who shall say what prospect life offers to another? Could a greater miracle take place than for us to look through each other's eyes for an instant? We should live in all the ages of the world in an hour; ay, in all the worlds of the ages. History, Poetry, Mythology!—I know of no reading of another's experience so startling and informing as this would be.

The greater part of what my neighbors call good I believe in my soul to be bad, and if I repent of anything, it is very likely to be my good behavior. What demon possessed me that I behaved so well? You may say the wisest thing you can, old man—you who have lived seventy years, not without honor of a kind—I hear an irresistible voice which invites me away from all that. One generation abandons the enterprises of another like stranded vessels.

I think that we may safely trust a good deal more than we do. We may waive just so much care of ourselves as we honestly bestow elsewhere. Nature is as well adapted to our weakness as to our strength. The incessant anxiety and strain of some is a well-nigh incurable form of disease. We are made to exaggerate the importance of what work we do; and yet how much is not done by us! or, what if we had been taken sick? How vigilant we are! determined not to live by faith if we can avoid it; all the day long on the alert, at night we unwillingly say our prayers and commit ourselves to uncertainties. So thoroughly and sincerely are we compelled to live, reverencing our life, and denying the possibility of change. This is the only way, we say; but there are as many ways as there can be drawn radii from one center. All change is a miracle to contemplate; but it is a miracle which is taking place every instant. Confucius said, "To know that we know what we know, and that we do not know what we do not know, that is true knowledge." When one man has reduced a fact of the imagination to be a fact to his understanding, I foresee that all men will at length establish their lives on that basis.

Let us consider for a moment what most of the trouble and anxiety which I have referred to is about, and how much it is necessary that we be troubled, or at least careful. It would be some advantage to live a primitive and frontier life, though in the midst of an outward civilization, if only to learn what are the gross necessaries of life and what methods have been taken to obtain them; or even to look over the old daybooks of the merchants, to see what it was that men most commonly bought at the stores, what they stored, that is, what are the grossest groceries. For the improvements of ages have had but little influence on the essential laws of man's existence: as our skeletons, probably, are not to be distinguished from those of our ancestors.

By the words, *necessary of life*, I mean whatever, of all that man obtains by his own exertions, has been from the first, or from long use has become, so important to human life that few, if any, whether from savageness, or poverty, or philosophy, ever attempt to do without it. To many creatures there is in this sense but one necessary of life, Food. To the bison of the prairie it is a few inches of palatable grass, with water to drink; unless he seeks the Shelter of the forest or the mountain's shadow. None of the brute creation requires more than Food and Shelter. The necessaries of life for man in this climate may, accurately enough, be distributed under the several heads of Food, Shelter, Clothing, and Fuel; for not till we have secured these are we prepared to entertain the true problems of life with freedom and a prospect of success. Man has invented not only houses but clothes and cooked food; and possibly from the accidental discovery of the warmth of fire, and the consequent use of it, at first a luxury, arose the present necessity to sit by it. We observe cats and dogs acquiring the same second nature. By proper Shelter and Clothing we legitimately retain our own internal heat; but with an excess of these, or of Fuel, that is, with an external heat greater than our own internal, may not cookery properly be said to begin? Darwin, the naturalist, says of the inhabitants of Tierra del Fuego, that while his own party, who were well clothed and sitting close to a fire, were far from too warm, these naked savages, who were farther off, were observed, to his great surprise, "to be steaming with perspiration at undergoing such a roasting." So, we are told, the New Hollander goes naked with impunity, while the European shivers in his clothes. Is it impossible to combine the hardiness of these savages with the intellectualness of the civilized man? According to Liebig, man's body is a stove, and food the fuel which keeps up the internal combustion in the lungs. In cold weather we eat more, in warm less. The animal heat is the result of a slow combustion, and disease and death take place when this is too rapid; or for want of fuel, or from some defect in the draught, the fire goes out. Of course the vital heat is not to be confounded with fire; but so much for analogy. It appears, therefore, from the above list, that the expression, *animal life*, is nearly synonymous with the expression, *animal heat*; for while Food may be regarded as the Fuel which keeps up the fire within us—and Fuel serves only to prepare that Food or to increase the warmth of our bodies by addition from without—Shelter and Clothing also serve only to retain the *heat* thus generated and absorbed.

The grand necessity, then, for our bodies, is to keep warm, to keep the vital heat in us. What pains we accordingly take, not only with our Food, and Clothing, and Shelter, but with our beds, which are our nightclothes, robbing the nests and breasts of birds to prepare this shelter within a shelter, as the mole has its bed of grass and leaves at the end of its burrow! The poor man is wont to complain that this is a cold world; and to cold, no less physical than social, we refer directly a great part of our ails. The summer, in some climates, makes possible to man a sort of Elysian life. Fuel, except to cook his Food, is then unnecessary; the sun is his fire, and many of the fruits are sufficiently cooked by its rays; while Food generally is more various, and more easily obtained, the Clothing and Shelter are wholly or half unnecessary. At the present day, and in this country, as I

23

find by my own experience, a few implements, a knife, an axe, a spade, a wheelbarrow, etc., and for the studious, lamplight, stationary, and access to a few books, rank next to necessaries, and can all be obtained as a trifling cost. Yet some, not wise, go to the other side of the globe, to barbarous and unhealthy regions, and devote themselves to trade for ten or twenty years, in order that they may live—that is, keep comfortably warm—and die in New England at last. The luxuriously rich are not simply kept comfortably warm, but unnaturally hot; as I implied before, they are cooked, of course á la mode.

Most of the luxuries, and many of the so-called comforts of life, are not only not indispensable, but positive hindrances to the elevation of mankind. With respect to luxuries and comforts, the wisest have ever lived a more simple and meager life than the poor. The ancient philosophers, Chinese, Hindu, Persian, and Greek, were a class than which none has been poorer in outward riches, none so rich in inward. We know not much about them. It is remarkable that *we* know so much of them as we do. The same is true of the more modern reformers and benefactors of their race. None can be an impartial or wise observer of human life but from the vantage ground of what *we* should call voluntary poverty. Of a life of luxury the fruit is luxury, whether in agriculture, or commerce, or literature, or art. There are nowadays professors of philosophy, but not philosophers. Yet it is admirable to profess because it was once admirable to live. To be a philosopher is not merely to have subtle thoughts, nor even to found a school, but so to love wisdom as to live according to its dictates, a life of simplicity, independence, magnanimity, and trust. It is to solve some of the problems of life, not only theoretically, but practically. The success of great scholars and thinkers is commonly a courtier-like success, not kingly, not manly. They make shift to live merely by conformity, practically as their fathers did, and are in no sense the progenitors of a nobler race of men. But why do men degenerate ever? What makes families run out? What is the nature of the luxury which enervates and destroys nations? Are we sure that there is none of it in our own lives? The philosopher is in advance of his age even in the outward form of his life. He is not fed, sheltered, clothed, warmed, like his contemporaries. How can a man be a philosopher and not maintain his vital heat by better methods than other men?

When a man is warmed by the several modes which I have described, what does he want next? Surely not more warmth of the same kind, as more and richer food, larger and more splendid houses, finer and more abundant clothing, more numerous, incessant, and hotter fires, and the like. When he has obtained those things which are necessary to life, there is another alternative than to obtain the superfluities; and that is, to adventure on life now, his vacation from humbler toil having commenced. The soil, it appears, is suited to the seed, for it has sent its radicle downward, and it may now send its shoot upward also with confidence. Why has man rooted himself thus firmly in the earth, but that he may rise in the same proportion into the heavens above?— for the nobler plants are valued for the fruit they bear at last in the air and light, far from the ground, and are not treated like the humbler esculents, which, though they may be biennials, are cultivated only till they have perfected their root, and often cut down at top for this purpose, so that most would not know them in their flowering season.

I do not mean to prescribe rules to strong and valiant natures, who will mind their own affairs whether in heaven or hell, and perchance build more magnificently and spend more lavishly then the richest, without ever impoverishing themselves, not knowing how they live—if, indeed, there are any such, as has been dreamed; nor to those who find their encouragement and inspiration in precisely the present condition of things, and cherish it with the fondness and enthusiasm of lovers—and, to some extent, I reckon myself in this number; I do not speak to those who are well employed, in whatever circumstances, and they know whether they are well employed or not; but mainly to the mass of men who are discontented, and idly complaining of the hardness of their lot or of the times, when they might improve them. There are some who complain most energetically and inconsolably of any, because they are, as they say, doing their duty. I also have in my mind that seemingly wealthy, but most terribly impoverished class of all, who have accumulated dross, but know not how to use it, or get rid of it, and thus have forged their own golden or silver fetters.

FOR DISCUSSION

1. Why does Thoreau describe inheriting property as a "misfortune"? (15)

2. According to Thoreau, why do most people go on living "lives of quiet desperation"? (18)

3. According to Thoreau, why do older people have little or nothing to teach younger ones?

4. Why does Thoreau say, "Most of the luxuries, and many of the so-called comforts of life, are not only not indispensable, but positive hindrances to the elevation of mankind"? (24)

FOR FURTHER REFLECTION

1. How applicable to contemporary society are Thoreau's ideas about work and possessions? What people or organizations today seem to be living by Thoreau's principles?

2. Do you agree with Thoreau when he says, "None can be an impartial or wise observer of human life but from the vantage ground of what *we* should call voluntary poverty"? (24)

Karl Marx (1818–1883) was born in Trier, Prussia (now Germany). He studied law, history, and philosophy at the universities of Bonn and Berlin and earned a doctorate from the University of Jena. In Berlin, he was introduced to the politically radical movements of the day. In the early 1840s, Marx wrote articles and became associate editor of a radical newspaper, and in 1843 he moved to Paris, where he met Friedrich Engels—the two developed a lifelong collaboration. They coauthored a number of works setting forth their materialistic concept of history, and were commissioned to write a political statement for the Communist League, a secret society they belonged to. This pamphlet, which articulated their theory of class struggle, became *The Communist Manifesto* (1848). Expelled from various countries, Marx moved to London in 1849, where he wrote *Das Kapital* (published in several volumes beginning in 1867). This selection is taken from Marx's *Economic and Philosophical Manuscripts of 1844.*

The Power of Money in Bourgeois Society

(selection)

By possessing the *property* of buying everything, by possessing the property of appropriating all objects, *money* is thus the *object* of eminent possession. The universality of its *property* is the omnipotence of its being. It therefore functions as the almighty being. Money is the *pimp* between man's need and the object, between his life and his means of life. But *that which* mediates *my* life for me, also *mediates* the existence of other people *for me*. For me it is the *other* person. . . .

That which is for me through the medium of *money*—that for which I can pay (i.e., that money can buy)—that am *I*, the possessor of the money. The extent of the power of money is the extent of my power. Money's properties are my properties and essential, powers—the properties and powers of its possessor. Thus, what I *am* and *am capable* of is by no means determined by my individuality. I am ugly, but I can buy for myself the most *beautiful* of women. Therefore I am not *ugly*, for the effect of *ugliness*—its deterrent power—is nullified by money. I, in my character as an individual, am *lame*, but money furnishes me with twenty-four feet. Therefore I am not lame. I am bad, dishonest, unscrupulous, stupid; but money is honored, and therefore so is its possessor. Money is the supreme good, therefore its possessor is good. Money, besides, saves me the trouble of being dishonest: I am therefore presumed honest. I am *stupid*, but money is the *real mind* of all things and how then should its possessor be stupid? Besides, he can buy talented people for himself, and is he who has power over the talented not more talented than the talented? Do not I, who thanks to money am capable of *all* that the human heart longs for, possess all human capacities? Does not my money therefore transform all my incapacities into their contrary?

If *money* is the bond binding me to *human* life, binding society to me, binding me and nature and man, is not money the bond of all *bonds*? Can it not dissolve and bind all ties? Is it not, therefore, the universal *agent of divorce*? It is the true *agent of divorce* as well as the true *binding agent*—the [universal] *galvano-chemical* power of Society. . . .

The overturning and confounding of all human and natural qualities, the fraternization of impossibilities—the *divine* power of money—lies in its *character* as men's estranged, alienating, and self-disposing *species-nature*. Money is the alienated *ability of mankind*.

That which I am unable to do as a *man*, and of which therefore all my individual essential powers are incapable, I am able to do by means of *money*. Money thus turns each of these powers into something that in itself it is not—turns it, that is, into its *contrary*.

If I long for a particular dish or want to take the mail coach because I am not strong enough to go by foot, money fetches me the dish and the mail coach: that is, it converts my wishes from something in the realm of imagination, translates them from their meditated, imagined, or willed existence into their *sensuous, actual* existence—from imagination to life, from imagined being into real being. In effecting this mediation, money is the *truly creative* power.

No doubt *demand* also exists for him who has no money, but his demand is a mere thing of the imagination without effect or existence for me, for a third party, for the others, and that therefore remains for me *unreal* and *objectless*. The difference between effective demand based on money and ineffective demand based on my need, my passion, my wish, etc., is the difference between *being* and *thinking*, between the imagined that *exists* merely within me and the imagined as it is for me outside me as a *real object*.

If I have no money for travel, I have no *need*—that is, no real and self-realizing need—to travel. If I have the *vocation* for study but no money for it, I have *no* vocation for study—that is, no *effective*, no *true* vocation. On the other hand, if I have really *no* vocation for study but have the will *and* the money for it, I have an *effective* vocation for it. Being the external, common *medium* and *faculty* for turning an *image* into *reality* and *reality* into a mere *image* (a faculty not springing from man as man or from human society as society), *money* transforms the *real essential powers of man and nature* into what are merely abstract conceits and therefore *imperfections*—into tormenting chimeras—just as it transforms r*eal imperfections and chimeras*—essential powers that are really impotent, that exist only in the imagination of the individual—into *real powers* and *faculties*.

In the light of this characteristic alone, money is thus the general overturning of *individualities* that turns them into their contrary and adds contradictory attributes to their attributes.

Money, then, appears as this *overturning* power both against the individual and against the bonds of society, etc., which claim to be *essences* in themselves. It transforms fidelity into infidelity, love into hate, hate into love, virtue into vice, vice into virtue, servant into master, master into servant, idiocy into intelligence and intelligence into idiocy.

Since money, as the existing and active concept of value, confounds and exchanges all things, it is the general *confounding* and *compounding* of all things —the world upside-down—the confounding and compounding of all natural and human qualities.

He who can buy bravery is brave, though a coward. As money is not exchanged for any one specific quality, for any one specific thing, or for any particular human essential power, but for the entire objective world of man and nature, from the standpoint of its possessor it therefore serves to exchange every property for every other, even contradictory, property and object: it is the fraternization of impossibilities. It makes contradictions embrace.

Assume *man* to be *man* and his relationship to the world to be a human one: then you can exchange love only for love, trust for trust, etc. If you want to enjoy art, you must be an artistically cultivated person; if you want to exercise influence over other people, you must be a person with a stimulating and encouraging effect on other people. Every one of your relations to man and to nature must be a *specific expression*, corresponding to the object of your will, of your *real individual* life. If you love without evoking love in return—that is, if your loving as loving does not produce reciprocal love; if through a *living expression* of yourself as a loving person you do not make yourself a *loved person*, then your love is impotent— a misfortune.

FOR DISCUSSION

1. Why does Marx say that in bourgeois society "that which is for me through the medium of *money*—that for which I can pay (i.e., that money can buy)—that am *I*, the possessor of the money"? (29)

2. How is it possible for money to be both "the bond of all *bonds*" and "the universal *agent of divorce*" between people? (30)

3. Does Marx think people can live free of the distorting and corrupting power of money?

4. At the end of his essay on money, why does Marx turn his attention to man's "human" relations to the world? (32)

FOR FURTHER REFLECTION

1. Do you agree with Marx that money essentially turns the world upside down and "makes contradictions embrace"? (32)

2. Based on the ideas in this text, why do you think many people from Marx's own time up until today have hated or feared Marxist philosophy?

Theodore Dreiser (1871–1945) was born in Terre Haute, Indiana, to a German immigrant father and a Mennonite mother. His best-known novels are *Sister Carrie* (1900) and *An American Tragedy* (1925). Dreiser is considered one of the pioneers of naturalism, a literary movement that uses realistic details to portray the shaping of human beings by the inescapable force of social conditions, heredity, and environment. He took on the social realities of American life in the early twentieth century, rejecting Victorian constraints. The publisher of *Sister Carrie*, once aware of the "immorality" of its story line, severely limited its advertising and distribution, and the novel's lack of success discouraged Dreiser from writing fiction for some years. It was finally republished in 1912. At a memorial service for Dreiser, noted journalist and critic H. L. Mencken said, "American writing, before and after his time, differed almost as much as biology before and after Darwin."

Sister Carrie
(selection)

The true meaning of money yet remains to be popularly explained and comprehended. When each individual realizes for himself that this thing primarily stands for and should only be accepted as a moral due—that it should be paid out as honestly stored energy, and not as a usurped privilege—many of our social, religious, and political troubles will have permanently passed. As for Carrie, her understanding of the moral significance of money was the popular understanding, nothing more. The old definition: "Money: something everybody else has and I must get," would have expressed her understanding of it thoroughly. Some of it she now held in her hand—two soft, green ten-dollar bills—and she felt that she was immensely better off for the having of them. It was something that was power in itself. One of her order of mind would have been content to be cast away upon a desert island with a bundle of money, and only the long strain of starvation would have taught her that in some cases it could have no value. Even then she would have had no conception of the relative value of the thing; her one thought would, undoubtedly, have concerned the pity of having so much power and the inability to use it.

The poor girl thrilled as she walked away from Drouet. She felt ashamed in part because she had been weak enough to take it, but her need was so dire, she was still glad. Now she would have a nice new jacket! Now she would buy a nice pair of pretty button shoes. She would get stockings, too, and a skirt, and, and—until already, as in the matter of her prospective salary, she had got beyond, in her desires, twice the purchasing power of her bills.

She conceived a true estimate of Drouet. To her, and indeed to all the world, he was a nice, goodhearted man. There was nothing evil in the fellow. He gave her the money out of a good heart—out of a realization of her want. He would not have given the same amount to a poor young man, but we must not forget that a poor young man could not, in the nature of things, have appealed to him like a poor young girl. Femininity affected his feelings. He was the creature of an inborn desire. Yet no beggar could have caught his eye and said, "My God, mister, I'm starving," but he would gladly have handed out what was considered the proper portion to give beggars and thought no more about it. There would have been no speculation, no philosophizing. He had no mental process in him worthy the dignity of either of those terms. In his good clothes and fine health, he was a merry, unthinking moth of the lamp. Deprived of his position, and struck by a few of the involved and baffling forces which sometimes play upon man he would have been as helpless as Carrie—as helpless, as nonunderstanding, as pitiable, if you will, as she.

Now, in regard to his pursuit of women, he meant them no harm, because he did not conceive of the relation which he hoped to hold with them as being harmful. He loved to make advances to women, to have them succumb to his charms, not because he was a cold-blooded, dark, scheming villain, but because his inborn desire urged him to that as a chief delight. He was vain, he was boastful, he was as deluded by fine clothes as any silly-headed girl. A truly deep-dyed villain could have hornswoggled him as readily as he could have flattered a pretty shopgirl. His fine success as a salesman lay in his geniality and the thoroughly reputable standing of his house. He bobbed about among men, a veritable bundle of enthusiasm—no power worthy the name of intellect, no thoughts worthy the adjective noble, no feelings long continued in one strain. A Madame Sappho would have called him a pig; a Shakespeare would have said "my merry child"; old, drinking Caryoe thought him a clever, successful businessman. In short, he was as good as his intellect conceived.

The best proof that there was something open and commendable about the man was the fact that Carrie took the money. No deep, sinister soul with ulterior motives could have given her fifteen cents under the guise of friendship. The unintellectual are not so helpless. Nature has taught the beasts of the field to fly when some unheralded danger threatens. She has put into the small, unwise head of the chipmunk the untutored fear of poisons. "He keepeth His creatures whole," was not written of beasts alone. Carrie was unwise, and, therefore, like the sheep in its unwisdom, strong in feeling. The instinct of self-protection, strong in all such natures, was roused but feebly, if at all, by the overtures of Drouet.

When Carrie had gone, he felicitated himself upon her good opinion. By George, it was a shame young girls had to be knocked around like that. Cold weather coming on and no clothes. Tough. He would go around to Fitzgerald and Moy's and get a cigar. It made him feel light of foot as he thought about her.

Carrie reached home in high good spirits, which she could scarcely conceal. The possession of the money involved a number of points which perplexed her seriously. How should she buy any clothes when Minnie knew that she had no money? She had no sooner entered the flat than this point was settled for her. It could not be done. She could think of no way of explaining.

"How did you come out?" asked Minnie, referring to the day.

Carrie had none of the small deception which could feel one thing and say something directly opposed. She would prevaricate, but it would be in the line of her feelings at least. So instead of complaining when she felt so good, she said:

"I have the promise of something."

"Where?"

"At the Boston Store."

"Is it sure promised?" questioned Minnie.

"Well, I'm to find out tomorrow," returned Carrie, disliking to draw out a lie any longer than was necessary.

Minnie felt the atmosphere of good feeling which Carrie brought with her. She felt now was the time to express to Carrie the state of Hanson's feeling about her entire Chicago venture.

"If you shouldn't get it—" she paused, troubled for an easy way.

"If I don't get something pretty soon, I think I'll go home."

Minnie saw her chance.

"Sven thinks it might be best for the winter, anyhow."

The situation flashed on Carrie at once. They were unwilling to keep her any longer, out of work. She did not blame Minnie, she did not blame Hanson very much. Now, as she sat there digesting the remark, she was glad she had Drouet's money.

"Yes," she said after a few moments, "I thought of doing that."

She did not explain that the thought, however, had aroused all the antagonism of her nature. Columbia City, what was there for her? She knew its dull, little round by heart. Here was the great, mysterious city which was still a magnet for her. What she had seen only suggested its possibilities. Now to turn back on it and live the little old life out there—she almost exclaimed against the thought.

She had reached home early and went in the front room to think. What could she do? She could not buy new shoes and wear them here. She would need to save part of the twenty to pay her fare home. She did not want to borrow of Minnie for that. And yet, how could she explain where she even got that money? If she could only get enough to let her out easy.

She went over the tangle again and again. Here, in the morning, Drouet would expect to see her in a new jacket, and that couldn't be. The Hansons expected her to go home, and she wanted to get away, and yet she did not want to go home. In the light of the way they would look on her getting money without work, the taking of it now seemed dreadful. She began to be ashamed. The whole situation depressed her. It was all so clear when she was with Drouet. Now it was all so tangled, so hopeless—much worse than it was before, because she had the semblance of aid in her hand which she could not use.

Her spirits sank so that at supper Minnie felt that she must have had another hard day. Carrie finally decided that she would give the money back. It was wrong to take it. She would go down in the morning and hunt for work. At noon she would meet Drouet as agreed and tell him. At this decision her heart sank, until she was the old Carrie of distress.

Curiously, she could not hold the money in her hand without feeling some relief. Even after all her depressing conclusions, she could sweep away all thought about the matter and then the twenty dollars seemed a wonderful and delightful thing. Ah, money, money, money! What a thing it was to have. How plenty of it would clear away all these troubles.

In the morning she got up and started out a little early. Her decision to hunt for work was moderately strong, but the money in her pocket, after all her troubling over it, made the work question the least shade less terrible. She walked into the wholesale district, but as the thought of applying came with each passing concern, her heart shrank. What a coward she was, she thought to herself. Yet she had applied so often. It would be the same old story. She walked on and on, and finally did go into one place, with the old result. She came out feeling that luck was against her. It was no use.

Without much thinking she reached Dearborn Street. Here was the great Fair store with its multitude of delivery wagons about, its long window display, its crowd of shoppers. It readily changed her thoughts, she who was so weary of them. It was here that she had intended to come and get her new things. Now for relief from distress, she thought she would go in and see. She would look at the jackets.

There is nothing in this world more delightful than that middle state in which we mentally balance at times, possessed of the means, lured by desire, and yet deterred by conscience or want of decision. When Carrie began wandering around the store amid the fine displays she was in this mood. Her original experience in this same place had given her a high opinion of its merits. Now she paused at each individual bit of finery, where before she had hurried on. Her woman's heart was warm with desire for them. How would she look in this, how charming that would make her! She came upon the corset counter and paused in rich reverie as she noted the dainty concoctions of color and lace there displayed. If she would only make up her mind, she could have one of those now. She lingered in the jewelry department. She saw the earrings, the bracelets, the pins, the chains. What would she not have given if she could have had them all! She would look fine too, if only she had some of these things.

The jackets were the greatest attraction. When she entered the store, she already had her heart fixed upon the peculiar little tan jacket with large mother-of-pearl buttons which was all the rage that fall. Still she delighted to convince herself that there was nothing she would like better. She went about among the glass cases and racks where these things were displayed, and satisfied herself that the one she thought of was the proper one. All the time she wavered in mind, now persuading herself that she could buy it right away if she chose, now recalling to herself the actual condition. At last the noon hour was dangerously near, and she had done nothing. She must go now and return the money.

Drouet was on the corner when she came up.

"Hello," he said, "where is the jacket and"—looking down—"the shoes?"

Carrie had thought to lead up to her decision in some intelligent way, but this swept the whole fore-schemed situation by the board.

"I came to tell you that—that I can't take the money."

"Oh, that's it, is it?" he returned. "Well, you come on with me. Let's go over here to Partridge's."

Carrie walked with him. Behold, the whole fabric of doubt and impossibility had slipped from her mind. She could not get at the points that were so serious, the things she was going to make plain to him.

"Have you had lunch yet? Of course you haven't. Let's go in here," and Drouet turned into one of the very nicely furnished restaurants off State Street, in Monroe.

"I mustn't take the money," said Carrie, after they were settled in a cozy corner, and Drouet had ordered the lunch. "I can't wear those things out there. They—they wouldn't know where I got them."

"What do you want to do," he smiled, "go without them?"

"I think I'll go home," she said, wearily.

"Oh, come," he said, "you've been thinking it over too long. I'll tell you what you do. You say you can't wear them out there. Why don't you rent a furnished room and leave them in that for a week?"

Carrie shook her head. Like all women, she was there to object and be convinced. It was for him to brush the doubts away and clear the path if he could.

"Why are you going home?" he asked.

"Oh, I can't get anything here."

"They won't keep you?" he remarked, intuitively.

"They can't," said Carrie.

"I'll tell you what you do," he said. "You come with me. I'll take care of you."

Carrie heard this passively. The peculiar state which she was in made it sound like the welcome breath of an open door. Drouet seemed of her own spirit and pleasing. He was clean, handsome, well dressed, and sympathetic. His voice was the voice of a friend.

"What can you do back at Columbia City?" he went on, rousing by the words in Carrie's mind a picture of the dull world she had left. "There isn't anything down there. Chicago's the place. You can get a nice room here and some clothes, and then you can do something."

Carrie looked out through the window into the busy street. There it was, the admirable, great city, so fine when you are not poor. An elegant coach, with a prancing pair of bays, passed by, carrying in its upholstered depths a young lady.

"What will you have if you go back?" asked Drouet. There was no subtle undercurrent to the question. He imagined that she would have nothing at all of the things he thought worthwhile.

Carrie sat still, looking out. She was wondering what she could do. They would be expecting her to go home this week.

Drouet turned to the subject of the clothes she was going to buy.

"Why not get yourself a nice little jacket? You've got to have it. I'll loan you the money. You needn't worry about taking it. You can get yourself a nice room by yourself. I won't hurt you."

Carrie saw the drift, but could not express her thoughts. She felt more than ever the helplessness of her case.

"If I could only get something to do," she said.

"Maybe you can," went on Drouet, "if you stay here. You can't if you go away. They won't let you stay out there. Now, why not let me get you a nice room? I won't bother you—you needn't be afraid. Then, when you get fixed up, maybe you could get something."

He looked at her pretty face and it vivified his mental resources. She was a sweet little mortal to him—there was no doubt of that. She seemed to have some power back of her actions. She was not like the common run of store girls. She wasn't silly,

In reality, Carrie had more imagination than he— more taste. It was a finer mental strain in her that made possible her depression and loneliness. Her poor clothes were neat, and she held her head unconsciously in a dainty way.

"Do you think I could get something?" she asked.

"Sure," he said, reaching over and filling her cup with tea. "I'll help you."

She looked at him, and he laughed reassuringly.

"Now I'll tell you what we'll do. We'll go over here to Partridge's and you pick out what you want. Then we'll look around for a room for you. You can leave the things there. Then we'll go to the show tonight."

Carrie shook her head.

"Well, you can go out to the flat then, that's all right. You don't need to stay in the room. Just take it and leave your things there."

She hung in doubt about this until the dinner was over.

"Let's go over and look at the jackets," he said.

Together they went. In the store they found that shine and rustle of new things which immediately laid hold of Carrie's heart. Under the influence of a good dinner and Drouet's radiating presence, the scheme proposed seemed feasible. She looked about and picked a jacket like the one which she had admired at The Fair. When she got it in her hand it seemed so much nicer. The saleswoman helped her on with it, and, by accident, it fitted perfectly. Drouet's face lightened as he saw the improvement. She looked quite smart.

"That's the thing," he said.

Carrie turned before the glass. She could not help feeling pleased as she looked at herself. A warm glow crept into her cheeks.

"That's the thing," said Drouet. "Now pay for it."

"It's nine dollars," said Carrie.

"That's all right—take it," said Drouet.

She reached in her purse and took out one of the bills. The woman asked if she would wear the coat and went off. In a few minutes she was back and the purchase was closed.

From Partridge's they went to a shoe store, where Carrie was fitted for shoes. Drouet stood by, and when he saw how nice they looked, said, "Wear them." Carrie shook her head, however. She was thinking of returning to the flat. He bought her a purse for one thing, and a pair of gloves for another, and let her buy the stockings.

"Tomorrow," he said, "you come down here and buy yourself a skirt."

In all of Carrie's actions there was a touch of misgiving. The deeper she sank into the entanglement, the more she imagined that the thing hung upon the few remaining things she had not done. Since she had not done these, there was a way out.

Drouet knew a place in Wabash Avenue where there were rooms. He showed Carrie the outside of these, and said: "Now, you're my sister." He carried the arrangement off with an easy hand when it came to the selection, looking around, criticizing, opining. "Her trunk will be here in a day or so," he observed to the landlady, who was very pleased.

When they were alone, Drouet did not change in the least. He talked in the same general way as if they were out in the street. Carrie left her things.

"Now," said Drouet, "why don't you move tonight?"

"Oh, I can't," said Carrie.

"Why not?"

"I don't want to leave them so."

He took that up as they walked along the avenue. It was a warm afternoon. The sun had come out and the wind had died down. As he talked with Carrie, he secured an accurate detail of the atmosphere of the flat.

"Come out of it," he said, "they won't care. I'll help you get along."

She listened until her misgivings vanished. He would show her about a little and then help her get something. He really imagined that he would. He would be out on the road and she could be working.

"Now, I'll tell you what you do," he said, "you go out there and get whatever you want and come away."

She thought a long time about this. Finally she agreed. He would come out as far as Peoria Street and wait for her. She was to meet him at half past eight. At half past five she reached home, and at six her determination was hardened.

"So you didn't get it?" said Minnie, referring to Carrie's story of the Boston Store.

Carrie looked at her out of the corner of her eye. "No," she answered.

"I don't think you'd better try anymore this fall," said Minnie.

Carrie said nothing.

When Hanson came home he wore the same inscrutable demeanour. He washed in silence and went off to read his paper. At dinner Carrie felt a little nervous. The strain of her own plans was considerable, and the feeling that she was not welcome here was strong.

"Didn't find anything, eh?" said Hanson.

"No."

He turned to his eating again, the thought that it was a burden to have her here dwelling in his mind. She would have to go home, that was all. Once she was away, there would be no more coming back in the spring.

Carrie was afraid of what she was going to do, but she was relieved to know that this condition was ending. They would not care. Hanson particularly would be glad when she went. He would not care what became of her.

After dinner she went into the bathroom, where they could not disturb her and wrote a little note.

"Goodbye, Minnie," it read. "I'm not going home. I'm going to stay in Chicago a little while and look for work. Don't worry. I'll be all right."

In the front room Hanson was reading his paper. As usual, she helped Minnie clear away the dishes and straighten up. Then she said:

"I guess I'll stand down at the door a little while." She could scarcely prevent her voice from trembling.

Minnie remembered Hanson's remonstrance.

"Sven doesn't think it looks good to stand down there," she said.

"Doesn't he?" said Carrie. "I won't do it anymore after this."

She put on her hat and fidgeted around the table in the little bedroom, wondering where to slip the note. Finally she put it under Minnie's hair-brush.

When she had closed the hall door, she paused a moment and wondered what they would think. Some thought of the queerness of her deed affected her. She went slowly down the stairs. She looked back up the lighted step, and then affected to stroll up the street. When she reached the corner she quickened her pace.

As she was hurrying away, Hanson came back to his wife.

"Is Carrie down at the door again?" he asked.

"Yes," said Minnie; "she said she wasn't going to do it anymore."

He went over to the baby where it was playing on the floor and began to poke his finger at it.

Drouet was on the corner waiting, in good spirits.

"Hello, Carrie," he said, as a sprightly figure of a girl drew near him. "Got here safe, did you? Well, we'll take a car."

FOR DISCUSSION

1. When she first accepts the two ten-dollar bills from Drouet, why does Carrie feel "immensely better off" and begin thinking about the new clothes she can buy? (35)

2. Why does Carrie decide that it was wrong to take the money from Drouet and that she must give it back? When she meets Drouet again, why is Carrie unable to keep to her decision to give the money back to him?

3. Why does Drouet rent a room for Carrie?

4. Does the narrator seem to have equal sympathy for Carrie and Drouet, or does he present one character more favorably than the other?

FOR FURTHER REFLECTION

1. Do you agree with Dreiser that understanding "the true meaning of money" would solve social problems? (35)

2. Under what circumstances is it possible to give or accept money without creating an obligation between people? Is it possible to give money completely unselfishly?

Zora Neale Hurston (1891–1960) was born in Notasulga, Alabama, and grew up in Eatonville, Florida, the first incorporated all-black town in the United States. She wrote novels, short stories, articles, an autobiography, and other nonfiction, and was a preeminent figure of the African American artistic and cultural movement known as the Harlem Renaissance. She graduated from Barnard College in 1928 with a degree in anthropology, and traveled throughout the Caribbean and the southern United States collecting folk tales. Her best-known work is *Their Eyes Were Watching God* (1937). Her autobiography, *Dust Tracks on a Road* (1942), brought Hurston acclaim, and she was on the faculty of North Carolina Central University. But eventually she faded from the public stage and she died in poverty in Florida. She was rediscovered in the 1970s, thanks in part to the efforts of a young Alice Walker, and today Hurston's work is widely read and studied.

The Gilded Six-Bits

It was a Negro yard around a Negro house in a Negro settlement that looked to the payroll of the G and G Fertilizer works for its support.

But there was something happy about the place. The front yard was parted in the middle by a sidewalk from gate to doorstep, a sidewalk edged on either side by quart bottles driven neck down into the ground on a slant. A mess of homey flowers planted without a plan but blooming cheerily from their helter-skelter places. The fence and house were whitewashed. The porch and steps scrubbed white.

The front door stood open to the sunshine so that the floor of the front room could finish drying after its weekly scouring. It was Saturday. Everything clean from the front gate to the privy house. Yard raked so that the strokes of the rake would make a pattern. Fresh newspaper cut in fancy edge on the kitchen shelves.

Missie May was bathing herself in the galvanized washtub in the bedroom. Her dark-brown skin glistened under the soapsuds that skittered down from her wash rag. Her stiff young breasts thrust forward aggressively like broad-based cones with the tips lacquered in black.

She heard men's voices in the distance and glanced at the dollar clock on the dresser.

"Humph! Ah'm way behind time t'day! Joe gointer be heah 'fore Ah git mah clothes on if Ah don't make haste."

She grabbed the clean meal sack at hand and dried herself hurriedly and began to dress. But before she could tie her slippers, there came the ring of singing metal on wood. Nine times.

Missie May grinned with delight. She had not seen the big tall man come stealing in the gate and creep up the walk grinning happily at the joyful mischief he was about to commit. But she knew that it was her husband throwing silver dollars in the door for her to pick up and pile beside her plate at dinner. It was this way every Saturday afternoon. The nine dollars hurled into the open door, he scurried to a hiding place behind the cape jasmine bush and waited.

Missie May promptly appeared at the door in mock alarm.

"Who dat chunkin' money in mah do'way?" she demanded. No answer from the yard. She leaped off the porch and began to search the shrubbery. She peeped under the porch and hung over the gate to look up and down the road. While she did this, the man behind the jasmine darted to the chinaberry tree. She spied him and gave chase.

"Nobody ain't gointer be chunkin' money at me and Ah not do 'em nothin'," she shouted in mock anger. He ran around the house with Missie May at his heels. She overtook him at the kitchen door. He ran inside but could not close it after him before she crowded in and locked with him in a rough and tumble. For several minutes the two were a furious mass of male and female energy. Shouting, laughing, twisting, turning, tussling, tickling each other in the ribs; Missie May clutching onto Joe and Joe trying, but not too hard, to get away.

"Missie May, take yo' hand out mah pocket!" Joe shouted out between laughs.

"Ah ain't, Joe, not lessen you gwine gimme whateve' it is good you got in yo' pocket. Turn it go, Joe, do Ah'll tear yo' clothes."

"Go on tear 'em. You de one dat pushes de needles round heah. Move yo' hand Missie May."

"Lemme git dat paper sack out yo' pocket. Ah bet its candy kisses."

"Tain't. Move yo' hand. Woman ain't go no business in a man's clothes nohow. Go way."

Missie May gouged way down and gave an upward jerk and triumphed.

"Unhhunh! Ah got it. It 'tis so candy kisses. Ah knowed you had somethin' for me in yo' clothes. Now Ah got to see whut's in every pocket you got."

Joe smiled indulgently and let his wife go through all of his pockets and take out the things that he had hidden there for her to find. She bore off the chewing gum, the cake of sweet soap, the pocket handkerchief as if she had wrested them from him, as if they had not been bought for the sake of this friendly battle.

"Whew! Dat play-fight done got me all warmed up," Joe exclaimed. "Got me some water in de kittle?"

"Yo' water is on de fire and yo' clean things is cross de bed. Hurry up and wash yo'self and git changed so we kin eat. Ah'm hongry." As Missie said this, she bore the steaming kettle into the bedroom.

"You ain't hongry, sugar," Joe contradicted her. "Youse jes' a little empty. Ah'm de one whut's hongry. Ah could eat up camp meetin', back off 'ssociation, and drink Jurdan dry. Have it on de table when Ah git out de tub."

"Don't you mess wid mah business, man. You git in yo' clothes. Ah'm a real wife, not no dress and breath. Ah might not look lak one, but if you burn me, you won't git a thing but wife ashes."

Joe splashed in the bedroom and Missie May fanned around in the kitchen. A fresh red and white checked cloth on the table. Big pitcher of buttermilk beaded with pale drops of butter from the churn. Hot fried mullet, crackling bread, ham hock atop a mound of string beans and new potatoes, and perched on the windowsill a pone of spicy potato pudding.

Very little talk during the meal but that little consisted of banter that pretended to deny affection but in reality flaunted it. Like when Missie May reached for a second helping of the tater pone. Joe snatched it out of her reach.

After Missie May had made two or three unsuccessful grabs at the pan, she begged, "Aw, Joe, gimme some mo' dat tater pone."

"Nope, sweetenin' is for us men-folks. Y'all pritty lil frail eels don't need nothin' lak dis. You too sweet already."

"Please, Joe."

"Naw, naw. Ah don't want you to git no sweeter than whut you is already. We goin' down de road a lil piece t'night so you go put on yo' Sunday-go-to-meetin' things."

Missie May looked at her husband to see if he was playing some prank. "Sho nuff, Joe?"

"Yeah. We goin' to de ice cream parlor."

"Where de ice cream parlor at, Joe?"

"A new man done come heah from Chicago and he done got a place and took and opened it up for a ice cream parlor, and bein' as it's real swell, Ah wants you to be one de first ladies to walk in dere and have some set down."

"Do Jesus, Ah ain't knowed nothin' 'bout it. Who de man done it?"

"Mister Otis D. Slemmons, of spots and places— Memphis, Chicago, Jacksonville, Philadelphia, and so on."

"Dat heavy-set man wid his mouth full of gold teethes?"

"Yeah, Where did you see 'im at?"

"Ah went down to de sto' tuh git a box of lye and Ah seen 'im standin' on de corner talkin' to some of de mens, and Ah come on back and went to scrubbin' de floor, and he passed and tipped his hat whilst Ah was scourin' de steps. Ah thought Ah never seen *him* befo'."

Joe smiled pleasantly. "Yeah, he's up to date. He got de finest clothes Ah ever seen on a colored man's back."

"Aw, he don't look no better in his clothes than you do in yourn. He got a puzzlegut on 'im and he so chuckle-headed, he got a pone behind his neck."

Joe looked down at his own abdomen and said wist-fully, "Wisht Ah had a build on me lak he got. He ain't puzzle-gutted, honey. He jes' got a corperation. Dat make 'm look lak a rich white man. All rich mens is got some belly on 'em."

"Ah seen de pitchers of Henry Ford and he's a spare-built man and Rockefeller look lak he ain't got but one gut. But Ford and Rockefeller and dis Slemmons and all de rest kin be as many-gutted as dey please, Ah'm satis-fied wid you jes' lak you is, baby. God took pattern after a pine tree and built you noble. Youse a pritty man, and if Ah knowed any way to make you mo' pritty still Ah'd take and do it."

Joe reached over gently and toyed with Missie May's ear. "You jes' say dat cause you love me, but Ah know Ah can't hold no light to Otis D. Slemmons. Ah ain't never been nowhere and Ah ain't got nothin' but you."

Missie May got on his lap and kissed him and he kissed back in kind. Then he went on. "All de womens is crazy 'bout 'im everywhere he go."

"How you know dat, Joe?"

"He tole us so hisself."

"Dat don't make it so. His mouf is cut crossways, ain't it? Well, he kin lie jes' lak anybody else."

"Good Lawd, Missie! You womens sho is hard to sense into things. He's got a five-dollar gold piece for a stickpin and he got a ten-dollar gold piece on his watch chain and his mouf is jes' crammed full of gold teethes. Sho wisht it wuz mine. And whut make it so cool, he got money 'cumulated. And womens give it all to 'im."

"Ah don't see whut de womens see on 'im. Ah wouldn't give 'im a wink if de sheriff wuz after 'im"

"Well, he tole us how de white womens in Chicago give 'im all dat gold money. So he don't 'low nobody to touch it at all. Not even put dey finger on it. Dey tole 'im not to. You kin make 'miration at it, but don't tetch it."

"Whyn't he stay up dere where dey so crazy 'bout 'im?"

"Ah reckon dey done made 'im vast-rich and he wants to travel some. He say dey wouldn't leave 'im hit a lick of work. He got mo' lady people crazy 'bout him than he kin shake a stick at."

"Joe, Ah hates to see you so dumb. Dat stray nigger jes' tell y'all anything and y'all b'lieve it."

"Go 'head on now, honey, and put on yo' clothes. He talkin' 'bout his pritty womens—Ah want 'im to see *mine*."

Missie May went off to dress and Joe spent the time trying to make his stomach punch out like Slemmons's middle. He tried the rolling swagger of the stranger, but found that his tall bone-and-muscle stride fitted ill with it. He just had time to drop back into his seat before Missie May came in dressed to go.

On the way home that night Joe was exultant. "Didn't Ah say ole Otis was swell? Can't he talk Chicago talk? Wuzn't dat funny whut he said when great big fat

ole Ida Armstrong come in? He asted me, 'Who is dat
broad wid de forte shake?' Dat's a new word. Us always
thought forty was a set of figgers but he showed us where
it means a whole heap of things. Sometimes he don't
say forty, he jes' say thirty-eight and two and dat mean
de same thing. Know whut he tole me when Ah wuz
payin' for our ice cream? He say, 'Ah have to hand it to
you, Joe. Dat wife of yours is jes' thirty-eight and two.
Yessuh, she's forte!' Ain't he killin'?"

"He'll do in case of a rush. But he sho is got uh heap
uh gold on 'im. Dat's de first time Ah ever seed gold
money. It lookted good on him sho nuff, but it'd look a
whole heap better on you,"

"Who, me? Missie May youse crazy! Where would a
po' man lak me git gold money from?"

Missie May was silent for a minute, then she said,
"Us might find some goin' long de road some time. Us
could."

"Who would be losin' gold money round heah? We
ain't even seen none dese white folks wearin' no gold
money on dey watch chain. You must be figgerin' Mister
Packard or Mister Cadillac goin' pass through heah."

"You don't know whut been lost 'round heah. Maybe
somebody way back in memorial times lost they gold
money and went on off and it ain't never been found. And
then if we wuz to find it, you could wear some 'thout
havin' no gang of womens lak dat Slemmons say he got."

Joe laughed and hugged her. "Don't be so wishful
'bout me. Ah'm satisfied de way Ah is. So long as Ah
be yo' husband. Ah don't keer 'bout nothin' else. Ah'd
ruther all de other womens in de world to be dead than
for you to have de toothache. Less we go to bed and git
our night rest."

It was Saturday night once more before Joe could
parade his wife in Slemmons's ice cream parlor again. He

worked the night shift and Saturday was his only night off. Every other evening around six o'clock he left home, and dying dawn saw him hustling home around the lake where the challenging sun flung a flaming sword from east to west across the trembling water.

That was the best part of life—going home to Missie May. Their whitewashed house, the mock battle on Saturday, the dinner and ice cream parlor afterwards, church on Sunday nights when Missie out-dressed any woman in town—all, everything was right.

One night around eleven the acid ran out at the G and G. The foreman knocked off the crew and let the steam die down. As Joe rounded the lake on his way home, a lean moon rode the lake in a silver boat. If anybody had asked Joe about the moon on the lake, he would have said he hadn't paid it any attention. But he saw it with his feelings. It made him yearn painfully for Missie. Creation obsessed him. He thought about children. They had been married for more than a year now. They had money put away. They ought to be making little feet for shoes. A little boy child would be about right.

He saw a dim light in the bedroom and decided to come in through the kitchen door. He could wash the fertilizer dust off himself before presenting himself to Missie May. It would be nice for her not to know that he was there until he slipped into his place in bed and hugged her back. She always liked that.

He eased the kitchen door open slowly and silently, but when he went to set his dinner bucket on the table he bumped it into a pile of dishes, and something crashed to the floor. He heard his wife gasp in fright and hurried to reassure her.

"Iss me, honey. Don't get skeered."

There was a quick, large movement in the bedroom. A rustle, a thud, and a stealthy silence. The light went out.

What? Robbers? Murderers? Some varmint attacking his helpless wife, perhaps. He struck a match, threw himself on guard, and stepped over the door sill into the bedroom.

The great belt on the wheel of Time slipped and eternity stood still. By the match light he could see the man's legs fighting with his breeches in his frantic desire to get them on. He had both chance and time to kill the intruder in his helpless condition—half in and half out of his pants—but he was too weak to take action. The shapeless enemies of humanity that live in the hours of Time had waylaid Joe. He was assaulted in his weakness. Like Samson awakening after his haircut. So he just opened his mouth and laughed.

The match went out and he struck another and lit the lamp. A howling wind raced across his heart, but underneath its fury he heard his wife sobbing and Slemmons pleading for his life. Offering to buy it with all that he had. "Please, suh, don't kill me. Sixty-two dollars at de sto'. Gold money."

Joe just stood. Slemmons looked at the window, but it was screened. Joe stood out like a rough-backed mountain between him and the door. Barring him from escape, from sunrise, from life.

He considered a surprise attack upon the big clown that stood there laughing like a chessy cat. But before his fist could travel an inch, Joe's own rushed out to crush him like a battering ram. Then Joe stood over him.

"Git into yo' damn rags, Slemmons, and dat quick."

Slemmons scrambled to his feet and into his vest and coat. As he grabbed his hat, Joe's fury overrode his intentions and he grabbed at Slemmons with his left hand and struck at him with his right. The right landed. The left grazed the front of his vest. Slemmons was knocked a somersault into the kitchen and fled through the open door. Joe found himself alone with Missie May, with the golden watch charm clutched in his left fist. A short bit of broken chain dangled between his fingers.

Missie May was sobbing. Wails of weeping without words. Joe stood, and after a while he found out that he had something in his hand. And then he stood and felt without thinking and without seeing with his natural eyes. Missie May kept on crying and Joe kept on feeling so much and not knowing what to do with all his feelings, he put Slemmons's watch charm in his pants pocket and took a good laugh and went to bed.

"Missie May, whut you cryin' for?"

"Cause Ah love you so hard and Ah know you don't love *me* no mo'."

Joe sank his face into the pillow for a spell then he said huskily, "You don't know de feelings of dat yet, Missie May."

"Oh Joe, honey, he said he wuz gointer give me dat gold money and he jes' kept on after me—"

Joe was very still and silent for a long time. Then he said, "Well, don't cry no mo', Missie May. Ah got yo' gold piece for you."

The hours went past on their rusty ankles. Joe still and quiet on one bed rail and Missie May wrung dry of sobs on the other. Finally the sun's tide crept upon the shore of night and drowned all its hours. Missie May with her face stiff and streaked toward the window saw the dawn come into her yard. It was day. Nothing more. Joe wouldn't be coming home as usual. No need to fling open the front door and sweep off the porch, making it nice for Joe. Never no more breakfast to cook; no more washing and starching of Joe's jumper-jackets and pants. No more nothing. So why get up?

With this strange man in her bed, she felt embarrassed to get up and dress. She decided to wait till he had dressed and gone. Then she would get up, dress quickly, and be gone forever beyond reach of Joe's looks and laughs. But he never moved. Red light turned to yellow, then white.

From beyond the no man's land between them came a voice. A strange voice that yesterday had been Joe's.

"Missie May, ain't you gonna fix me no breakfus'?"

She sprang out of bed. "Yeah, Joe. Ah didn't reckon you wuz hongry."

No need to die today. Joe needed her for a few more minutes anyhow.

Soon there was a roaring fire in the cookstove. Water bucket full and two chickens killed. Joe loved fried chicken and rice. She didn't deserve a thing and good Joe was letting her cook him some breakfast. She rushed hot biscuits to the table as Joe took his seat.

He ate with his eyes in his plate. No laughter, no banter.

"Missie May, you ain't eatin' yo' breakfus'."

"Ah don't choose none, Ah thank yuh."

His coffee cup was empty. She sprang to refill it. When she turned from the stove and bent to set the cup beside Joe's plate, she saw the yellow coin on the table between them.

She slumped into her seat and wept into her arms.

Presently Joe said calmly, "Missie May, you cry too much. Don't look back lak Lot's wife aud turn to salt."

The sun, the hero of every day, the impersonal old man that beams as brightly on death as on birth, came up every morning and raced across the blue dome and dipped into the sea of fire every evening. Water ran downhill and birds nested.

Missie knew why she didn't leave Joe. She couldn't. She loved him too much, but she could not understand why Joe didn't leave her. He was polite, even kind at times, but aloof.

There were no more Saturday romps. No ringing silver dollars to stack beside her plate. No pockets to rifle. In fact the yellow coin in his trousers was like a monster hiding in the cave of his pockets to destroy her.

She often wondered if he still had it, but nothing could have induced her to ask nor yet to explore his pockets to see for herself. Its shadow was in the house whether or no.

One night Joe came home around midnight and complained of pains in the back. He asked Missie to rub him down with liniment. It had been three months since Missie had touched his body and it all seemed strange. But she rubbed him. Graceful for the chance. Before morning, youth triumphed and Missie exulted. But the next day, as she joyfully made up their bed, beneath her pillow she found the piece of money with the bit of chain attached.

Alone to herself, she looked at the thing with loathing, but look she must. She took it into her hands with trembling and saw first thing that it was no gold piece. It was a gilded half dollar. Then she knew why Slemmons had forbidden anyone to touch his gold. He trusted village eyes at a distance not to recognize his stickpin as a gilded quarter, and his watch charm as a four-bit piece.

She was glad at first that Joe had left it there. Perhaps he was through with her punishment. They were man and wife again. Then another thought came clawing at her. He had come home to buy from her as if she were any woman in the long house. Fifty cents for her love. As if to say that he could pay as well as Slemmons. She slid the coin into his Sunday pants pocket and dressed herself and left his house.

Halfway between her house and the quarters she met her husband's mother, and after a short talk she turned and went back home. Never would she admit defeat to that woman who prayed for it nightly. If she had not the substance of marriage she had the outside show. Joe must leave *her*. She let him see she didn't want his old gold four-bits too.

She saw no more of the coin for some time though she knew that Joe could not help finding it in his pocket. But his health kept poor, and he came home at least every ten days to be rubbed.

The sun swept around the horizon, trailing its robes of weeks and days. One morning as Joe came in from work, he found Missie May chopping wood. Without a word he took the ax and chopped a huge pile before he stopped.

"You ain't got no business choppin' wood, and you know it."

"How come? Ah been choppin' it for de last longest."

"Ah ain't blind. You makin' feet for shoes."

"Won't you be glad to have a lil baby chile, Joe?"

"You know dat 'thout astin' me."

"Iss gointer be a boy chile and de very spit of you."

"You reckon, Missie May?"

"Who else could it look lak?"

Joe said nothing, but he thrust his hand deep into his pocket and fingered something there.

It was almost six months later Missie May took to bed and Joe went and got his mother to come wait on the house.

Missie May delivered a fine boy. Her travail was over when Joe came in from work one morning. His mother and the old women were drinking great bowls of coffee around the fire in the kitchen.

The minute Joe came into the room his mother called him aside.

"How did Missie May make out?" he asked quickly.

"Who, dat gal? She strong as a ox. She gointer have plenty mo'. We done fixed her wid de sugar and lard to sweeten her for de nex' one."

Joe stood silent awhile.

"You ain't ast 'bout de baby, Joe. You oughter be mighty proud cause he sho is de spittin' image of yuh, son. Dat's yourn all right, if you never git another one, dat un is yourn. And you know Ah'm mighty proud too, son, cause Ah never thought well of you marryin' Missie May cause her ma used tuh fan her foot round right smart and Ah been mighty skeered dat Missie May wuz gointer git misput on her road."

Joe said nothing. He fooled around the house till late in the day then just before he went to work, he went and stood at the foot of the bed and asked his wife how she felt. He did this every day during the week.

On Saturday he went to Orlando to make his market. It had been a long time since he had done that.

Meat and lard, meal and flour, soap and starch. Cans of corn and tomatoes. All the staples. He fooled around town for a while and bought bananas and apples. Way after while he went around to the candy store.

"Hellow, Joe," the clerk greeted him. "Ain't seen you in a long time."

"Nope, Ah ain't been heah. Been round in spots and places."

"Want some of them molasses kisses you always buy?"

"Yessuh." He threw the gilded half dollar on the counter. "Will dat spend?"

"Whut is it, Joe? Well, I'll be doggone! A gold-plated four-bit piece. Where'd you git it, Joe?"

"Offen a stray nigger dat come through Eatonville. He had it on his watch chain for a charm—goin' round making out iss gold money. Ha ha! He had a quarter on his tiepin and it wuz all golded up too. Tryin' to fool people. Makin' out he so rich and everything. Ha! Ha! Tryin' to tole off folkses wives from home."

"How did you git it, Joe? Did he fool you, too?"

"Who, me? Naw suh! He ain't fooled me none. Know whut Ah done? He come round me wid his smart talk. Ah hauled off and knocked 'im down and took his old four-bits way from 'im. Gointer buy my wife some good ole lasses kisses wid it. Gimme fifty cents worth of dem candy kisses."

"Fifty cents buys a mightly lot of candy kisses, Joe. Why don't you split it up and take some chocolate bars, too. They eat good, too."

"Yessuh, dey do, but Ah wants all dat in kisses. Ah got a lil boy chile home now. Tain't a week old yet, but he kin suck a sugar tit and maybe eat one them kisses hisself."

Joe got his candy and left the store. The clerk turned to the next customer. "Wisht I could be like these darkies. Laughin' all the time. Nothin worries 'em."

Back in Eatonville, Joe reached his own front door. There was the ring of singing metal on wood. Fifteen times. Missie May couldn't run to the door, but she crept there as quickly as she could.

"Joe Banks, Ah hear you chunkin' money in mah do'way. You wait till Ah got mah strength back and Ah'm gointer fix you for dat."

FOR DISCUSSION

1. Why does Joe throw the silver dollars in the doorway every Saturday?

2. Does Missie May have sex with Otis T. Slemmons only for the money?

3. Why does Joe leave the gold coin under Missie May's pillow the first time they make love again after she has been with Slemmons?

4. Why does Joe tell the store clerk the story about knocking down the man with the coin and taking it from him?

FOR FURTHER REFLECTION

1. What is Hurston saying about love and money when Slemmons's "gold" coins turn out to be only gilded common coins?

2. Why are people sometimes willing to betray even those they love for money? Under what circumstances should someone be forgiven for such a betrayal?

John Cheever (1912–1982), born in Quincy, Massachusetts, was an American fiction writer best known for his short stories, almost all of which were first published in the *New Yorker*. He also published several novels, including *The Wapshot Chronicle* (1957), *The Wapshot Scandal* (1964), *Bullet Park* (1969), and *Falconer* (1977). Cheever used precise observation and straightforward language to explore post–World War II upper-middle-class suburbia—dubbed "Cheever country" by some literary critics. His characters tend to be successful but unfulfilled people who struggle against society's expectations in their longing for personal satisfaction. Cheever won the National Book Award for *The Wapshot Chronicle* and the Pulitzer Prize for *The Stories of John Cheever* (1978). Toward the end of his life he said, "Literature is the only continuous and coherent account of our struggle to be illustrious, a monument of aspiration, a vast pilgrimage."

The Housebreaker of Shady Hill

My name is Johnny Hake. I'm thirty-six years old, stand five feet eleven in my socks, weigh one hundred and forty-two pounds stripped, and am, so to speak, naked at the moment and talking into the dark. I was conceived in the Hotel St. Regis, born in the Presbyterian Hospital, raised on Sutton Place, christened and confirmed in St. Bartholomew's, and I drilled with the Knickerbocker Greys, played football and baseball in Central Park, learned to chin myself on the framework of East Side apartment-house canopies, and met my wife (Christina Lewis) at one of those big cotillions at the Waldorf. I served four years in the Navy, have four kids now, and live in a *banlieue* called Shady Hill. We have a nice house with a garden and a place outside for cooking meat, and on summer nights, sitting there with the kids and looking into the front of Christina's dress as she bends over to salt the steaks, or just gazing at the lights in heaven, I am as thrilled as I am thrilled by more hardy and dangerous pursuits, and I guess this is what is meant by the pain and sweetness of life.

I went to work right after the war for a parablendeum manufacturer, and seemed on the way to making this my life. The firm was patriarchal; that is, the old man would start you on one thing and then switch you to another, and he had his finger in every pie—the Jersey mill and the processing plant in Nashville—and behaved as if he had wool-gathered the whole firm during a catnap. I stayed out of the old man's way as nimbly as I could, and behaved in his presence as if he had shaped me out of clay with his own hands and breathed the fire of life into me. He was the kind despot who needed a front, and this was Gil Bucknam's job. He was the old man's right hand, front, and peacemaker, and he could garnish any deal with the humanity the old man lacked, but he started staying out of the office—at first for a day or two, then for two weeks, and then for longer. When he returned, he would complain about stomach trouble or eyestrain, although anyone could see that he was looped. This was not so strange, since hard drinking was one of the things he had to do for the firm. The old man stood it for a year and then came into my office one morning and told me to get up to Bucknam's apartment and give him the sack.

This was as devious and dirty as sending an office boy to can the chairman of the board. Bucknam was my superior and my senior by many years, a man who condescended to do so whenever he bought me a drink, but this was the way the old man operated, and I knew what I had to do. I called the Bucknam apartment, and Mrs. Bucknam said that I could see Gil that afternoon. I had lunch alone and hung around the office until about three, when I *walked* from our midtown office to the Bucknams' apartment, in the East Seventies. It was early in the fall—the World Series was being played—and a thunderstorm was entering the city. I could hear the noise of big guns and smell the rain when I got to the Bucknams' place. Mrs. Bucknam let me in, and all the troubles of that past year seemed to be in her face, hastily concealed by a thick coat of powder. I've never seen such burned-out eyes, and she was wearing one of those old-fashioned garden-party dresses with big flowers on it. (They had three kids in college, I knew, and a schooner with a hired hand, and many other expenses.) Gil was in bed, and Mrs. Bucknam let me into the bedroom. The storm was about to break now, and everything stood in a gentle half darkness so much like dawn that it seemed as if we should be sleeping and dreaming, and not bringing one another bad news.

Gil was jolly and lovable and condescending, and said that he was *so* glad to see me; he had bought a lot of presents for my children when he was last in Bermuda and had forgotten to mail them. "Would you get those things, darling?" he asked. "Do you remember where we put them?" Then she came back into the room with five or six large and expensive-looking packages and unloaded them into my lap,

I think of my children mostly with delight, and I love to give them presents. I was charmed. It was a ruse, of course—hers, I guessed—and one of many that she must have thought up over the last year to hold their world together. (The wrappings were not fresh, I could see, and when I got home and found in them some old cashmere sweaters that Gil's daughters had not taken to college and a Scotch cap with a soiled sweatband, it only deepened my feeling of sympathy for the Bucknams in their trouble.) With a lap full of presents for my kiddies and sympathy leaking out of every joint, I couldn't give him the ax. We talked about the World Series and about some small matters at the office, and when the rain and the wind began, I helped Mrs. Bucknam shut the windows in the apartment, and then I left and took an early train home through the storm. Five days later, Gil Bucknam went on the wagon for good, and came back to the office to sit again at the right hand of the old man, and my skin was one of the first he went after. It seemed to me that if it had been my destiny to be a Russian ballet dancer, or to make art jewelry, or to paint *Schuhplattler* dancers on bureau drawers and landscapes on clamshells and live in some very low-tide place like Provincetown, I wouldn't

71

have known a queerer bunch of men and women than I knew in the parablendeum industry, and I decided to strike out on my own.

My mother taught me never to speak about money when there was a shirtful, and I've always been very reluctant to speak about it when there was any scarcity, so I cannot paint much of a picture of what ensued in the next six months. I rented office space—a cubicle with a desk and a phone was what it amounted to—and sent out letters, but the letters were seldom answered and the telephone might just as well have been disconnected, and when it came time to borrow money, I had nowhere to turn. My mother hated Christina, and I don't think she can have much money, in any case, because she never bought me an overcoat or a cheese sandwich when I was a kid without telling me that it came out of her principal. I had plenty of friends, but if my life depended on it I couldn't ask a man for a drink and touch him for five hundred—and I needed more. The worst of it was that I hadn't painted anything like an adequate picture to my wife.

I thought about this one night when we were dressing to go to dinner up the road at the Warburtons'. Christina was sitting at her dressing table putting on earrings. She is a pretty woman in the prime of life, and her ignorance of financial necessity is complete. Her neck is graceful, her breasts gleamed as they rose in the cloth of her dress, and, seeing the decent and healthy delight she took in her own image, I could not tell her that we were broke. She had sweetened much of my life, and to watch her seemed to freshen the wellsprings of some clear energy in me that made the room and the pictures on the wall and the moon that I could see outside the window all vivid and cheerful. The truth would make her cry and ruin her make-up and the Warburtons' dinner party for her, and she would sleep in the guest room. There seemed to be as much truth in her beauty and the power she exerted over my senses as there was in the fact that we were overdrawn at the bank.

The Warburtons are rich, but they don't mix; they may not even care. She is an aging mouse, and he is the kind of man that you wouldn't have liked at school. He has a bad skin and rasping voice and a fixed idea—lechery. The Warburtons are always spending money, and that's what you talk about with them. The floor of their front hall is black-and-white marble from the old Ritz, and their cabanas at Sea Island are being winterized, and they are flying to Davos for ten days, and buying a pair of saddle horses, and building a new wing. We were late that night, and the Meserves and the Chesneys were already there, but Carl Warburton hadn't come home, and Sheila was worried. "Carl has to walk through a terrible slum to get to the station," she said, "and he carries thousands of dollars on him, and I'm so afraid he'll be *victimized*. . . ." Then Carl came home and told a dirty story to the mixed company, and we went in to dinner. It was the kind of party where everybody has taken a shower and put on their best clothes, and where some old cook has been peeling mushrooms or picking the meat out of crab shells since daybreak. I wanted to have a good time. That was my wish, but my wishes could not get me off the ground that night. I felt as if I was at some god-awful birthday party of my childhood that my mother had brought me to with threats and promises. The party broke up at about half past eleven, and we went home. I stayed out in the garden finishing one of Carl Warburton's cigars. It was a Thursday night, and my checks wouldn't bounce until Tuesday, but I had to do something soon. When I went upstairs, Christina was asleep, and I fell asleep myself, but I woke again at about three.

I had been dreaming about wrapping bread in colored parablendeum Filmex. I had dreamed a full-page spread in a national magazine: BRING SOME COLOR INTO YOUR BREADBOX! The page was covered with jewel-toned loaves of bread—turquoise bread, ruby bread, and bread the color of emeralds. In my sleep the idea had seemed to me like a good one; it had cheered me, and it was a letdown to find myself in the dark bedroom. Feeling sad then, I thought about all the loose ends of my life, and this brought me around to my old mother, who lives alone in a hotel in Cleveland. I saw her getting dressed to go down and have dinner in the hotel dining room. She seemed pitiable, as I imagined her—lonely and among strangers. And yet, when she turned her head, I saw that she still had some biting teeth left in her gums.

She sent me through college, arranged for me to spend my vacations in pleasant landscapes, and fired my ambitions, such as they are, but she bitterly opposed my marriage, and our relations have been strained ever since. I've often invited her to come and live with us, but she always refuses, and always with bad feeling. I send her flowers and presents, and write her every week, but these attentions only seem to fortify her conviction that my marriage was a disaster for her and for me. Then I thought about her apron strings, for when I was a kid, she seemed to be a woman whose apron strings were thrown across the Atlantic and the Pacific oceans; they seemed to be looped, like vapor trails, across the very drum of heaven. I thought of her now without rebellion or anxiety—only with sorrow that all our exertions should have been rewarded with so little clear emotion, and that we could not drink a cup of tea together without stirring up all kinds of bitter feeling. I longed to correct this, to reenact the whole relationship with my mother against a more simple and human background, where the cost of my education would not have come so high in morbid emotion. I wanted to do it all over again in some emotional Arcadia, and have us both behave differently, so that I could think of her at three in the morning without guilt, and so that she would be spared loneliness and neglect in her old age.

I moved a little closer to Christina and, coming into the area of her warmth, suddenly felt all kindly and delighted with everything, but she moved in her sleep, away from me. Then I coughed. I coughed again. I coughed loudly. I couldn't stop coughing, and I got out of bed and went into the dark bathroom and drank a glass of water. I stood at the bathroom window and looked down into the garden. There was a little wind. It seemed to be changing its quarter. It sounded like a dawn wind—the air was filled with a showery sound— and felt good on my face. There were some cigarettes on the back of the toilet, and I lit one in order to get back to sleep. But when I inhaled the smoke, it hurt my lungs, and I was suddenly convinced that I was dying of bronchial cancer.

I have experienced all kinds of foolish melancholy— I've been homesick for countries I've never seen, and longed to be what I couldn't be—but all these moods were trivial compared to my premonition of death. I tossed my cigarette into the toilet (ping) and straightened my back, but the pain in my chest was only sharper, and I was convinced that the corruption had begun. I had friends who would think of me kindly, I knew, and Christina and the children would surely keep alive an affectionate memory. But then I thought about money again, and the Warburtons, and my rubber checks approaching the clearinghouse, and it seemed to me that money had it all over love. I had yearned for some women—turned green, in fact—but it seemed to me that I had never yearned for anyone the way I yearned that night for money. I went to the closet in our bedroom and put on some old blue sneakers and a pair of pants and a dark pullover. Then I went downstairs and out of the house. The moon had set, and there were not many stars, but the air above the trees and hedges was full of dim light. I went around the Trenholmes' garden then, gumshoeing over the grass, and down the lawn to the Warburtons' house. I listened for sounds from the open windows, and all I heard was the ticking of a clock. I went up the front steps and opened the screen door and started across the floor from the old Ritz. In the dim night light that came in at the windows, the house looked like a shell, a nautilus, shaped to contain itself.

I heard the noise of a dog's license tag, and Sheila's old cocker came trotting down the hall. I rubbed him behind the ears, and then he went back to wherever his bed was, grunted, and fell asleep. I knew the plan of the Warburtons' house as well as I knew the plan of my own. The staircase was carpeted, but I first put my foot on one of the treads to see if it creaked. Then I started up the stairs. All the bedroom doors stood open, and from Carl and Sheila's bedroom, where I had often left my coat at big cocktail parties, I could hear the sound of deep breathing. I stood in the doorway for a second to take my bearings. In the dimness I could see the bed, and a pair of pants and a jacket hung over the back of a chair. Moving swiftly, I stepped into the room and took a big billfold from the inside pocket of the coat and started back to the hall. The violence of my emotions may have made me clumsy, because Sheila woke. I heard her say, "Did you hear that noise, darling?" "S'wind," he mumbled, and then they were quiet again. I was safe in the hall—safe from everything but myself. I seemed to be having a nervous breakdown out there. All my saliva was gone, the lubricants seemed to drain out of my heart, and whatever the juices were that kept my legs upright were going. It was only by holding on to the wall that I could make any progress at all. I clung to the banister on my way down the stairs, and staggered out of the house.

Back in my own dark kitchen, I drank three or four glasses of water. I must have stood by the kitchen sink for a half hour or longer before I thought of looking in Carl's wallet. I went into the cellarway and shut the cellar door before I turned the light on. There was a little over nine hundred dollars. I turned the light off and went back into the dark kitchen. Oh, I never knew that a man could be so miserable and that the mind could open up so many chambers and fill them with self-reproach! Where were the trout streams of my youth, and other innocent pleasures? The wet-leather smell of the loud waters and the keen woods after a smashing rain; or at opening day the summer breezes smelling like the grassy breath of Holsteins—your head would swim—and all the brooks full then (or so I imagined, in the dark kitchen) of trout, our sunken treasure. I was crying.

Shady Hill, as I say, a *banlieue* and open to criticism by city planners, adventurers, and lyric poets, but if you work in the city and have children to raise, I can't think of a better place. My neighbors are rich, it is true, but riches in this case mean leisure, and they use their time wisely. They travel around the world, listen to good music, and given a choice of paper books at an airport, will pick Thucydides, and sometimes Aquinas. Urged to build bomb shelters, they plant trees and roses, and their gardens are splendid and bright. Had I looked, the next morning, from my bathroom window into the evil-smelling ruin of some great city, the shock of recalling what I had done might not have been so violent, but the moral bottom had dropped out of my world without changing a mote of sunlight. I dressed stealthily—for what child of darkness would want to hear the merry voices of his family?—and caught an early train. My gabardine suit was meant to express cleanliness and probity, but I was a miserable creature whose footsteps had been mistaken for the noise of the wind. I looked at the paper. There had been a thirty-thousand-dollar payroll robbery in the Bronx. A White Plains matron had come home from a party to find her furs and jewelry gone. Sixty thousand dollars' worth of medicine had been taken from a warehouse in Brooklyn. I felt better at discovering how common the thing I had done was. But only a little better, and only for a short while. Then I was faced once more with the realization that I was a common thief and an impostor, and that I had done something so reprehensible that it violated the tenets of every known religion. I had stolen, and what's more, I had criminally entered the house of a friend and broken all the unwritten laws that held the community together. My conscience worked so on my spirits—like the hard beak of a carnivorous bird—that my left eye began to twitch, and again I seemed on the brink of a general nervous collapse. When the train reached the city, I went to the bank. Leaving the bank, I was nearly hit by a taxi. My anxiety was not for my bones but for the fact that Carl Warburton's wallet might be found in my pocket. When I thought no one was looking, I wiped the wallet on my trousers (to remove the finger-prints) and dropped it into the ash can.

I thought that coffee might make me feel better, and went into a restaurant, and sat down at a table with a stranger. The soiled lace-paper doilies and half-empty glasses of water had not been taken away, and at the stranger's place there was a thirty-five-cent tip, left by an earlier customer. I looked at the menu, but out of the corner of my eye I saw the stranger pocket the thirty-five-cent tip. What a crook! I got up and left the restaurant.

I walked into my cubicle, hung up my hat and coat, sat down at my desk, shot my cuffs, sighed, and looked into space, as if a day full of challenge and decision were about to begin. I hadn't turned on the light. In a little while, the office beside mine was occupied, and I heard my neighbor clear his throat, cough, scratch a match, and settle down to attack the day's business.

The walls were flimsy—part frosted glass and part plywood—and there was no acoustical privacy in these offices. I reached into my pocket for a cigarette with as much stealth as I had exercised at the Warburtons', and waited for the noise of a truck passing on the street outside before I lit a match. The excitement of eavesdropping took hold of me. My neighbor was trying to sell uranium stock over the telephone. His line went like this: First he was courteous. Then he was nasty. "What's the matter, Mr. X? Don't you want to make any money?" Then he was *very* scornful. "I'm sorry to have bothered you, Mr. X. I thought you *had* sixty-five dollars to invest." He called twelve numbers without any takers. I was as quiet as a mouse. Then he telephoned the information desk at Idlewild, checking the arrival of planes from Europe. London was on time. Rome and Paris were late. "No, he ain't in yet," I heard him say to someone over the phone. "It's dark in there." My heart was beating fast. Then my telephone began to ring, and I counted twelve rings before it stopped. "I'm positive, I'm positive," the man in the next office said. "I can hear his telephone ringing, and he ain't answering it, and he's just a lonely son of a bitch looking for a job. Go ahead, go ahead, I tell you. I ain't got time to get over there. Go ahead. . . . Seven, eight, three, five, seven, seven. . . ." When he hung up, I went to the door, opened and closed it, turned the light on, rattled the coat hangers, whistled a tune, sat down heavily at my desk chair, and dialed the first telephone number that came to my mind. It was an old friend—Burt Howe—and he exclaimed when he heard my voice. "Hakie, I been looking for you everywhere! You sure folded up your tents and stole away."

"Yes," I said.

"Stole away," Howe repeated. "Just stole away. But what I wanted to talk with you about is this deal I thought you might be interested in. It's a one-shot, but it won't take you more than three weeks. It's a steal, They're green, and they're dumb, and they're loaded, and it's just like stealing."

"Yes," I said.

"Well, then, can you meet me for lunch at Cardin's at twelve-thirty, and I'll give you the details?" Howe asked.

"O.K.," I said hoarsely. "Thanks a lot, Burt."

"We went out to the shack on Sunday," the man in the next office was saying as I hung up. "Louise got bit by a poisonous spider. The doctor gave her some kind of injection. She'll be all right." He dialed another number and began, "We went out to the shack on Sunday. Louise got bit by a poisonous spider . . ."

It was possible that a man whose wife had been bitten by a spider and who found some time on his hands might call three or four friends and tell them about it, and it was equally possible that the spider might be a code of warning or of assent to some unlawful traffic. What frightened me was that by becoming a thief I seemed to have surrounded myself with thieves and operators.

My left eye had begun to twitch again, and the inability of one part of my consciousness to stand up under the reproach that was being heaped into it by another part made me cast around desperately for someone else who could be blamed. I had read often enough in the papers that divorce sometimes led to crime. My parents were divorced when I was about five. This was a good clue and quickly led me on to something better.

My father went to live in France after the divorce, and I didn't see him for ten years. Then he wrote Mother for permission to see me, and she prepared me for this reunion by telling me how drunken, cruel, and lewd the old man was. It was in the summer, and we were on Nantucket, and I took the steamer alone, and went to New York on the train. I met my father at the Plaza early in the evening, but not so early that he hadn't begun to drink. With the long, sensitive nose of an adolescent I smelled the gin on his breath, and I noticed that he bumped into a table and sometimes repeated himself. I realized later that this reunion must have been strenuous for a man of sixty, which he was. We had dinner and then went to see *The Roses of Picardy*. As soon as the chorus came on, Father said that I could have any one of them that I wanted; the arrangements were all made. I could even have one of the specialty dancers. Now, if I'd felt that he had crossed the Atlantic to perform this service for me, it might have been different, but I felt he'd made the trip in order to do a disservice to my mother. I was scared. The show was in one of those old-fashioned theatres that appear to be held together with angels. Brown-gold angels held up the ceiling; they held up the boxes; they even seemed to hold up the balcony with about four hundred people in it. I spent a lot of time looking at those dusty gold angels. If the ceiling of the theatre had fallen on my head, I would have been relieved. After the show, we went back to the hotel to wash before meeting the girls, and the old man stretched out on the bed for a minute and began to snore. I picked his wallet of fifty dollars, spent the night at Grand Central, and took an early morning train to Woods Hole. So the whole thing was explained, including the violence of the emotion I had experienced in the Warburtons' upstairs hall; I had been reliving that scene at the Plaza. It had not been my fault that I had stolen then, and it had not been my fault when I went to the Warburtons'. It was my father's fault! Then I remembered that my father was buried in Fontainebleau fifteen years ago, and could be nothing much more now than dust.

I went into the men's room and washed my hands and face, and combed my hair down with a lot of water. It was time to go out for lunch. I thought anxiously of the lunch ahead of me, and, wondering why, was astonished to realize that it was Burt Howe's free use of the word "steal." I hoped he wouldn't keep on saying it.

Even as the thought floated across my mind in the men's room, the twitching in my eye seemed to spread over my cheek; it seemed as if this verb were embedded in the English language like a poisoned fishhook. I had committed adultery, and the word "adultery" had no force for me; I had been drunk, and the word "drunkenness" had no extraordinary power. It was only "steal" and all its allied nouns, verbs, and adverbs that had the power to tyrannize over my nervous system, as if I had evolved, unconsciously, some doctrine wherein the act of theft took precedence over all the other sins in the Decalogue and was a sign of moral death.

The sky was dark when I came out on the street. Lights were burning everywhere. I looked into the faces of the people that I passed for some encouraging signs of honesty in such a crooked world, and on Third Avenue I saw a young man with a tin cup, holding his eyes shut to impersonate blindness. That seal of blindness, the striking innocence of the upper face, was betrayed by the frown and the crow's-feet of a man who could see his drinks on the bar. There was another blind beggar on Forty-First Street, but I didn't examine his eye sockets, realizing that I couldn't assess the legitimacy of every beggar in the city.

Cardin's is a men's restaurant in the Forties. The stir and bustle in the vestibule only made me feel retiring, and the hatcheck girl, noticing, I suppose, the twitch in my eye, gave me a very jaded look.

Burt was at the bar, and when we had ordered our drinks, we got down to business. "For a deal like this, we ought to meet in some back alley," he said, "but a fool and his money *and* so forth. It's three kids. P. J. Burdette is one of them, and they've got a cool million between them to throw away. Someone's bound to steal from them, so it may as well be you." I put my hand over the left side of my face to cover the tic. When I tried to raise my glass to my mouth, I spilled gin all over my suit. "They're all three of them just out of college," Burt said. "And they've all three of them got so much in the kitty that even if you picked them clean they wouldn't feel any pain. Now, in order to participate in this burglary, all you have to do . . ."

The toilet was at the other end of the restaurant, but I got there. Then I drew a basin of cold water and stuck my head and face into it. Burt had followed me to the washroom. As I was drying myself with a paper towel, he said, "You know, Hakie, I wasn't going to mention it, but now that you've been sick, I may as well tell you that you look awful. I mean, from the minute I saw you I knew something was wrong. I just want to tell you that whatever it is—sauce or dope or trouble at home—it's a lot later than you think, and maybe you should be doing something about it. No hard feelings?" I said that I was sick, and waited in the toilet long enough for Burt to make a getaway. Then I got my hat and another jaded look from the hatcheck girl, and saw in the afternoon paper on a chair by the checkroom that some bank robbers in Brooklyn had got away with eighteen thousand dollars.

I walked around the streets, wondering how I would shape up as a pickpocket and bag snatcher, and all the arches and spires of St. Patrick's only reminded me of poor boxes. I took the regular train home, looking out of the window at a peaceable landscape and a spring evening, and it seemed to me fishermen and lone bathers and grade-crossing watchmen and sandlot ball players and lovers unashamed of their sport and the owners of small sailing craft and old men playing pinochle in firehouses were the people who stitched up the big holes in the world that were made by men like me.

Now Christiana is the kind of woman who, when she is asked by the alumnae secretary of her college to describe her status, gets dizzy thinking about the variety of her activities and interests. And what, on a given day, stretching a point here and there, does she have to do? Drive me to the train. Have the skis repaired. Book a tennis court. Buy the wine and groceries for the monthly dinner of the Société Gastronomique du Westchester Nord. Look up some definitions in Larousse. Attend a League of Women Voters symposium on sewers. Go to a full-dress lunch for Bobsie Neil's aunt. Weed the garden. Iron a uniform for the part-time maid. Type two and a half pages of her paper on the early novels of Henry James. Empty the wastebaskets. Help Tabitha prepare the children's supper. Give Ronnie some batting practice. Put her hair in pin curls. Get the cook. Meet the train. Bathe. Dress. Greet her guests in French at half past seven. Say *bonsoir* at eleven. Lie in my arms until twelve. Eureka! You might say that she is prideful, but I think only that she is a woman enjoying herself in a country that is prosperous and young. Still, when she met me at the train that night, it was difficult for me to rise to all this vitality.

It was my bad luck to have to take the collection at early Communion on Sunday, although I was in no condition. I answered the pious looks of my friends with a very crooked smile and then knelt by a lancet-shaped stained-glass window that seemed to be made from the butts of vermouth and Burgundy bottles. I knelt on an imitation-leather hassock that had been given by some guild or auxiliary to replace one of the old, snuff-colored hassocks, which had begun to split at the seams and show bits of straw, and made the whole place smell like an old manger. The smell of straw and flowers, and the vigil light, and the candles flickering in the rector's breath, and the damp of this poorly heated stone building were all as familiar to me and belonged as much to my early life as the sounds and smells of a kitchen or a nursery, and yet they seemed, that morning, to be so potent that I felt dizzy. Then I heard, in the baseboard on my right, a rat's tooth working like an auger in the hard oak. "Holy, Holy, Holy," I said very loudly, hoping to frighten the rat. "Lord God of hosts, Heaven and earth are FULL of Thy Glory!" The small congregation muttered its amens with a sound like a footstep, and the rat went on scraping away at the baseboard. And then—perhaps because I was absorbed in the noise of the rat's tooth, or because the smell of dampness and straw was soporific—when I looked up from the shelter I had made of my hands,

I saw the rector drinking from the chalice and realized that I had missed Communion.

At home, I looked through the Sunday paper for other thefts, and there were plenty. Banks had been looted, hotel safes had been emptied of jewelry, maids and butlers had been tied to kitchen chairs, furs and industrial diamonds had been stolen in job lots, delicatessens, cigar stores, and pawnshops had been broken into, and someone had stolen a painting from the Cleveland Institute of Art. Late in the afternoon, I raked leaves. What could be more contrite than cleaning the lawn of the autumn's dark rubbish under the streaked, pale skies of spring?

While I was raking leaves, my sons walked by. "The Toblers are having a softball game," Ronnie said. "*Everybody's* there."

"Why don't you play?" I asked,

"You can't play unless you've been invited," Ronnie said over his shoulder, and then they were gone. Then I noticed that I could hear the cheering from the softball game to which we had not been invited. The Toblers lived down the block. The spirited voices seemed to sound clearer and clearer as the night came on; I could even hear the noise of ice in glasses, and the voices of the ladies raised in a feeble cheer.

Why hadn't I been asked to play softball at the Toblers'? I wondered. Why had we been excluded from these simple pleasures, this lighthearted gathering, the fading laughter and voices and slammed doors of which seemed to gleam in the darkness as they were withdrawn from my possession? Why wasn't *I* asked to play softball at the Toblers'? Why should social aggrandizement—*climbing*, really—exclude a nice guy like me from a softball game? What kind of a world was that? Why should I be left alone with my dead leaves in the twilight—as I was—feeling so forsaken, lonely, and forlorn that I was chilled?

If there is anybody I detest, it is weak-minded sentimentalists—all those melancholy people who, out of an excess of sympathy for others, miss the thrill of their own essence and drift through life without identity, like a human fog, feeling sorry for everyone. The legless beggar in Times Square with his poor display of pencils, the rouged old lady in the subway who talks to herself, the exhibitionist in the public toilet, the drunk who has dropped on the subway stairs, do more than excite their pity; they are at a glance transformed into these unfortunates. Derelict humanity seems to trample over their unrealized souls, leaving them at twilight in a condition closely resembling the scene of a prison riot. Disappointed in themselves, they are always ready to be disappointed for the rest of us, and they will build whole cities, whole creations, firmaments and principalities, of tear-wet disappointment. Lying in bed at night, they will think tenderly of the big winner who lost his parimutuel ticket, of the great novelist whose magnum opus was burned mistakenly for trash, and of Samuel Tilden, who lost the presidency of the United States through the shenanigans of the electoral college. Detesting this company, then, it was doubly painful for me to find myself in it. And, seeing a bare dogwood tree in the starlight, I thought, How sad everything is!

Wednesday was my birthday. I recalled this fact in the middle of the afternoon, at the office, and the thought that Christina might be planning a surprise party brought me in one second from a sitting to a standing position, breathless. Then I decided that she wouldn't. But just the preparations the children would make presented an emotional problem; I didn't see how I could face it.

I left the office early and had two drinks before I took the train. Christina looked pleased with everything when she met me at the station, and I put a very good face on my anxiety. The children had changed into clean clothes, and wished me a happy birthday so fervently that I felt awful. At the table there was a pile of small presents, mostly things the children had made—cuff links out of buttons, and a memo pad, and so forth. I thought I was very bright, considering the circumstances, and pulled my snapper, put on my silly hat, blew out the candles on the cake, and thanked them all, but then it seemed that there was another present—my *big* present—and after dinner I was made to stay inside while Christina and the children went outside, and then Juney came in and led me outdoors and around in back of the house, where they all were. Leaning against the house was an aluminum extension ladder with a card and a ribbon tied to it, and I said, as if I'd been hit, "What in *hell* is the meaning of this?"

"We thought you'd need it, Daddy," Juney said.

"What would I ever need a ladder for? What do you think I am—a second-story worker?"

"Storm windows," Juney said. "Screens—"

I turned to Christina. "Have I been talking in my sleep?"

"No," Christina said. "You haven't been talking in your sleep."

Juney began to cry.

"You could take the leaves out of the rain gutters," Ronnie said. Both of the boys were looking at me with long faces.

"Well, you must admit it's a very unusual present," I said to Christina.

"*God!*" Christina said. "Come on, children. Come on." She herded them in at the terrace door.

I kicked around the garden until after dark. The lights went on upstairs. Juney was still crying, and Christina was singing to her. Then she was quiet. I waited until the lights went on in our bedroom, and after a little while I climbed the stairs. Christina was in a nightgown, sitting at her dressing table, and there were heavy tears in her eyes.

"You'll have to try and understand," I said.

"I couldn't possibly. The children have been saving for months to buy you that damned-fool contraption."

"You don't know what I've been through," I said.

"If you'd been through hell, I wouldn't forgive you," she said. "You haven't been through anything that would justify your behavior. They've had it hidden in the garage for a week. They're so *sweet*."

"I haven't felt like myself," I said.

"Don't tell *me* that you haven't felt like yourself," she said. "I've looked forward to having you leave in the morning, and I've dreaded having you come home at night."

"I can't have been all that bad," I said.

"It's been hell," she said. "You've been sharp with the children, nasty to me, rude to your friends, and malicious behind their backs. It's been hideous."

"Would you like me to go?"

"Oh, Lord, would I like you to go! Then I could breathe."

"What about the children?"

"Ask my lawyer."

"I'll go, then,"

I went down the hall to the closet where we keep the bags. When I took out my suitcase, I found that the children's puppy had chewed the leather binding loose all along one side. Trying to find another suitcase, I brought the whole pile down on top of me, boxing my ears. I carried my bag with this long strip of leather trailing behind me back into our bedroom. "*Look*," I said. "Look at this, Christina. The dog has chewed the binding off my suitcase." She didn't even raise her head. "I've poured twenty thousand dollars a year into this establishment for ten years," I shouted, "and when the time comes for me to go, I don't even have a decent suitcase! Everybody else has a suitcase. Even the cat has a nice traveling bag," I threw open my shirt drawer, and there were only four clean shirts. I don't have enough clean shirts to last a week!" I shouted. Then I got a few things together, clapped my hat on my head, and marched out. I even thought, for a minute, of taking the car, and I went into the garage and looked it over. Then I saw the FOR SALE sign that had been hanging on the house when we bought it long, long ago. I wiped the dirt off the sign and got a nail and a rock and went around to the front of the house and nailed the FOR SALE sign onto a maple tree. Then I walked to the station. It's about a mile. The long strip of leather was trailing along behind me, and I stopped and tried to rip it off the suitcase, but it wouldn't come. When I got down to the station, I found there wasn't another train until four in the morning. I decided I would wait. I sat down on my suitcase and waited five minutes. Then I marched home again. Halfway there I saw Christina coming down the street, in a sweater and a skirt and sneakers—the quickest things to put on, but, summery things—and we walked home together and went to bed.

On Saturday, I played golf, and although the game finished late, I wanted to take a swim in the club pool before I went home. There was no one at the pool but Tom Maitland. He is a dark-skinned and nice-looking man, very rich, but quiet. He seems withdrawn. His wife is the fattest woman in Shady Hill, and nobody much likes his children, and I think he is the kind of man whose parties and friendship and affairs in love and business all rest like an intricate superstructure—a tower of matchsticks—on the melancholy of his early youth. A breath could bring the whole thing down. It was nearly dark when I had finished swimming; the clubhouse was lighted and you could hear the sounds of dinner on the porch. Maitland was sitting at the edge of the pool dabbling his feet in the bright-blue water, with its Dead Sea smell of chlorine. I was drying myself off, and as I passed him, I asked if he wasn't going in. "I don't know how to swim," he said. He smiled and looked away from me then to the still, polished water of the pool, in the dark landscape. "We used to have a pool at home," he said, "but I never got a chance to swim in it. I was always studying the violin." There he was, forty-five years old and at least a millionaire, and he couldn't even float, and I don't suppose he had many occasions to speak as honestly as he had just spoken. While I was getting dressed, the idea settled in my head—with no help from me—that the Maitlands would be my next victims.

A few nights later, I woke up at three. I thought over the loose ends in my life—Mother in Cleveland, and parablendeum—and then I went into the bathroom to light a cigarette before I remembered that I was dying of bronchial cancer and leaving my widow and orphans penniless. I put on my blue sneakers and the rest of the outfit, looked in at the open doors of the children's rooms, and then went out. It was cloudy. I walked through back gardens to the corner. Then I crossed the street and turned up the Maitlands' driveway, walking on the grass at the edge of the gravel. The door was open, and I went in, just as excited and frightened as I had been at the Warburtons' and feeling insubstantial in the dim light—a ghost. I followed my nose up the stairs to where I knew their bedroom was, and, hearing heavy breathing and seeing a jacket and some pants on a chair, I reached for the pocket of the jacket, but there wasn't one. It wasn't a suit coat at all; it was one of those bright satin jackets that kids wear. There was no sense in looking for a wallet in *his* trousers. He couldn't make that much cutting the Maitlands' grass. I got out of there in a hurry.

I did not sleep any more that night but sat in the dark thinking about Tom Maitland, and Gracie Maitland, and the Warburtons, and Christina, and my own sordid destiny, and how different Shady Hill looked at night than in the light of day.

But I went out the next night—this time to the Pewters', who were not only rich but booze fighters, and who drank so much that I didn't see how they could hear thunder after the lights were turned out. I left, as usual, a little after three.

I was thinking sadly about my beginnings—about how I was made by a riggish couple in a midtown hotel after a six-course dinner with wines, and my mother had told me so many times that if she hadn't drunk so many old-fashioneds before that famous dinner I would still be unborn on a star. And I thought about my old man and that night at the Plaza and the bruised thighs of the peasant women of Picardy and all the brown-gold angels that held the theatre together and my terrible destiny. While I was walking toward the Pewters', there was a harsh stirring in all the trees and gardens, like a draft on a bed of fire, and I wondered what it was until I felt the rain on my hands and face, and then I began to laugh.

I wish I could say that a kindly lion had set me straight, or an innocent child, or the strains of distant music from some church, but it was no more than the rain on my head—the smell of it flying up to my nose—that showed me the extent of my freedom from the bones in Fontainebleau and the works of a thief. There were ways out of my trouble if I cared to make use of them. I was not trapped. I was here on earth because I chose to be. And it was no skin off my elbow how I had been given the gifts of life so long as I possessed them, and I possessed them then—the tie between the wet grass roots and the hair that grew out of my body, the thrill of my mortality that I had known on summer nights, loving the children, and looking down the front of Christina's dress. I was standing in front of the Pewters' by this time, and I looked up at the dark house and then turned and walked away. I went back to bed and had pleasant dreams. I dreamed I was sailing a boat on the Mediterranean. I saw some worn marble steps leading down into the water, and the water itself—blue, saline, and dirty. I stepped the mast, hoisted the sail, and put my hand on the tiller. But why, I wondered as I sailed away, should I seem to be only seventeen years old? But you can't have everything.

It is not, as somebody once wrote, the smell of corn bread that calls us back from death; it is the lights and signs of love and friendship. Gil Bucknam called me the next day and said that the old man was dying and would I come back to work; I went to see him, and he explained that it was the old man who was after my skin, and, of course, I was glad to come home to parablendeum.

What I did not understand, as I walked down Fifth Avenue that afternoon, was how a world that had seemed so dark could, in a few minutes. become so sweet. The sidewalks seemed to shine, and, going home on the train, I beamed at those foolish girls who advertise girdles on the signboards in the Bronx. I got an advance on my salary the next morning, and, taking some precautions about fingerprints, I put nine hundred dollars into an envelope and walked over to the Warburtons' when the last lights in the neighborhood had been put out. It had been raining, but the rain had let up. The stars were beginning to show. There was no sense in overdoing prudence, and I went around to the back of their house, found the kitchen door open, and put the envelope on a table in the dark room. As I was walking away from the house, a police car drew up beside me. and a patrolman I know cranked down the window and asked, "What are you doing out at this time of night, Mr. Hake?"

"I'm walking the dog," I said cheerfully. There was no dog in sight, but they didn't look. "Here, Toby! Here, Toby! Here, Toby! *Good* dog!" I called, and off I went, whistling merrily in the dark.

FOR DISCUSSION

1. Why does Johnny Hake steal from the Warburtons instead of telling his wife about their financial situation or asking for help from anyone?

2. Why does stealing trouble Johnny's conscience so greatly, when drunkenness and adultery have not?

3. When Johnny goes to the office after stealing from the Warburtons, why does he suddenly feel surrounded by "thieves and operators"? (80)

4. At the end of the story, why does feeling the rain make Johnny think that "there were ways out of my trouble if I cared to make use of them"? (93)

FOR FURTHER REFLECTION

1. What is Cheever saying about modern suburban life by having Johnny Hake struggle internally with his actions and motivations while no one around him seems to suspect what he is going through?

2. At the end of the story, has Johnny Hake found a better way to live? In what ways, if any, has he changed?

Barbara Ehrenreich (1941–) was born in Butte, Montana. Though both her BA and PhD are in the sciences, she became a social critic and journalist, writing essays, articles, and books about subjects that fascinate her. She is a passionate activist in the areas of health care, peace, women's rights, and economic justice. She is best known for *Nickel and Dimed: On (Not) Getting By in America* (2001) and is the author of many other books, including *Fear of Falling: The Inner Life of the Middle Class* (1989), which was nominated for a National Book Critics' Circle Award; and *Bright-Sided* (2009), which explores the positive-thinking movement in America. In *Nickel and Dimed*, the author takes on various jobs to find out what it is like to live in the United States as a low-wage, unskilled worker. In the following excerpt, she reports on her experiences in retail sales in Minnesota.

Selling in Minnesota
(selection)

I decide there must be something I am doing wrong, some cue I am missing. Budgie's owners had been confident that Apartment Search would find me a place. When I call another friend of a friend, a professor at a college in St. Paul who has briefed me on the Twin Cities' industrial history, he concedes to being aware of an affordable-housing "crisis" but has no idea what I should do. Those rental agents who are kind enough to talk to me all recommend the same thing: find a motel that rents by the week and stay there until something opens up.[1] So, through multiple calls, I arrive at a list of eleven motels in the Twin Cities area, all of them of the non-brand-name variety, offering weekly rates. The rates, though, are not anybody's definition of "affordable," ranging from $200 a week at the Hill View in Shakopee to $295 at the Twin Lakes in southern Minneapolis, and many of these places are full. I head for the Hill View, which wants a $60 cash deposit. I drive and I drive. I go off the map, I leave suburbs and

1. The last few years have seen a steady decline in the number of affordable apartments nationwide. In 1991 there were forty-seven affordable rental units available to every one hundred low-income families, while in 1997 there were only thirty-six such units for every one hundred families ("Rental Housing Assistance—The Worsening Crisis: A Report to Congress on Worst-Case Housing Needs," Housing and Urban Development Department, March 2000). No national—or even reliable local—statistics are available, but apparently more and more of the poor have been reduced to living in motels. Census takers

commercial strips far behind, I enter the open fields, which make for a nice change, drivingwise—but to live in? The vicinity of the Hill View contains no diners, no fast-food joints or grocery stores, no commercial establishments at all except for a couple of agricultural-equipment warehouses. The distance is unacceptable; as is the room, when I get to see it: no microwave, no fridge, hardly any space not occupied by the bed. And what would I do if I didn't feel like being in bed—invite myself in for a tour of the Caterpillar parts warehouse?

Twin Lakes (not its real name) is at least in Minneapolis. There the East Indian owner tells me that all his residents are long-term, working people and that I can have a room on the second floor, where I won't have to keep the drapes shut during the day for privacy. Again, no fridge or microwave. Weakly, I tell him I'll take it and will move in in a couple of days. No problem. He even waives the deposit. But I have a bad feeling about the place, partly because everything looks gray and stained and partly because there's a deranged-looking guy hanging out by the coin-op washer-dryer who follows me with bloodshot blue eyes.

On the job front, though, things are moving along briskly. I had been told at Menards to show up for "orientation" at ten o'clock Wednesday morning, and since I assume that my being hired is conditional on passing

---

distinguish between standard motels, such as those that tourists stay in, and residential motels, which rent on a weekly basis, usually to long-term tenants. But many motels contain mixed populations or change from one type to the other depending on the season. Long-term motel residents are almost certainly undercounted, since motel owners often deny access to census takers and residents themselves may be reluctant to admit they live in motels, crowded in with as many as four people or more in a room (Willoughby Mariano, "The Inns and Outs of the Census," *Los Angeles Times*, May 22, 2000).

the drug test, I call to confirm the appointment. Yes, they're expecting me—I hope not just for the purpose of denouncing me as a chemical misfit. But the orientation is friendly and upbeat. Lee-Ann, a worn-looking blonde in her forties, and I sit across a table from Walt, who lays out the main points in a jolly, offhand way: Be nice to the guests, even when they get irate because they can't return things, and they're always trying to return things. Don't be absent without calling in. Watch out for a certain top manager, who hits on women when he visits the store and generally acts like "a shit." We will need to wear belts, to which a knife (for opening cardboard boxes, I suppose) and a tape measure will be attached, and the cost of these items, which he pushes across the table to us, will be deducted from our first paycheck. And oh yes, we will be getting "little presents" now and then—ballpoint pens, coffee mugs, T-shirts promoting seasonal items. Then Walt hands us our vests and our ID badges, and I am touched to see that he has made up two for me, one with "Barbara" and another with "Barb." I can take my choice.

When Walt leaves the room for a moment, I turn to Lee-Ann and say, "Does this mean we're hired?" Because it seems odd to me that no offer has been made or accepted. "Looks like," she says, and tells me that she hasn't even taken her drug test. She went to the testing place, but she didn't have any photo ID because her wallet was stolen, and of course they wouldn't test her without photo ID. Then Walt comes back and takes me out on the floor to meet Steve, a "really great guy," who will be my supervisor in plumbing. But here, on the sales floor, doubt rushes in. The shelves of plumbing equipment, and there seem to be acres of them, contain not a single item I can name, which gives me an idea of what it feels like to be aphasic. Would I be able to get by with pointing and grunting? Steve's smile seems more like a smirk, as if he's reading my mind and finding not a speck of plumbing knowledge lodged within it. Start Friday, he says, shift is noon to eleven. I think I haven't heard him right, nor can I quite believe the wage Walt tells me I'll be getting—not $8.50 but an incredible $10 an hour,

Now I don't need Wal-Mart anymore, I think, although it turns out they need me. Roberta calls to tell me, in fulsome tones, that my "drug screen is fine" and that I'm due in tomorrow at three for orientation. The test result does not have the desired effect of making me feel absolved or even clean. In fact I feel irritated and can't help wondering whether I could have gotten the same result without spending $30 and three days on detox and bloat. I ask her what the pay is—it should be noted that she does not offer this information herself—and when she says $7 an hour, I think: OK, case closed. But I decide, in the spirit of caution and inquiry, to attend the Wal-Mart orientation anyway. This turns out, for unforeseen physiological reasons, to be another major mistake.

For sheer grandeur, scale, and intimidation value, I doubt if any corporate orientation exceeds that of Wal-Mart. I have been told that the process will take eight hours, which will include two fifteen-minute breaks and one half-hour break for a meal, and will be paid for like a regular shift. When I arrive, dressed neatly in khakis and clean T-shirt, as befits a potential Wal-Mart "associate," I find there are ten new hires besides myself, mostly young and Caucasian, and a team of three, headed by Roberta, to do the "orientating." We sit around a long table in the same windowless room where I was interviewed, each with a thick folder of paperwork in front of us, and hear Roberta tell once again about raising six children, being a "people person,"

discovering that the three principles of Wal-Mart philosophy were the same as her own, and so on. We begin
with a video, about fifteen minutes long, on the history
and philosophy of Wal-Mart, or, as an anthropological
observer might call it, the Cult of Sam. First young
Sam Walton, in uniform, comes back from the war. He
starts a store, a sort of five-and-dime; he marries and
fathers four attractive children; he receives a Medal of
Freedom from President Bush, after which he promptly
dies, making way for the eulogies. But the company goes
on, yes indeed. Here the arc of the story soars upward
unstoppably, pausing only to mark some fresh mile-
stone of corporate expansion. 1992: Wal-Mart becomes
the largest retailer in the world. 1997: Sales top $100
billion. 1998: The number of Wal-Mart associates hits
825,000, making Wal-Mart the largest private employer
in the nation. Each landmark date is accompanied by a
clip showing throngs of shoppers, swarms of associates,
or scenes of handsome new stores and their adjoining
parking lots. Over and over we hear in voiceover or
see in graphic display the "three principles," which are
maddeningly, even defiantly, nonparallel: "respect for
the individual, exceeding customers' expectations, strive
for excellence."

"Respect for the individual" is where we, the associates, come in, because vast as Wal-Mart is, and tiny
as we may be as individuals, everything depends on
us. Sam always said, and is shown saying, that "the
best ideas come from the associates"—for example, the
idea of having a "people greeter," an elderly employee
(excuse me, associate) who welcomes each customer
as he or she enters the store. Three times during the
orientation, which began at three and stretches to nearly
eleven, we are reminded that this brainstorm originated
in a mere associate, and who knows what revolutions in

retailing each one of us may propose? Because our ideas are welcome, more than welcome, and we are to think of our managers not as bosses but as "servant-leaders," serving us as well as the customers. Of course, all is not total harmony, in every instance, between associates and their servant-leaders. A video on "associate honesty" shows a cashier being caught on videotape as he pockets some bills from the cash register. Drums beat ominously as he is led away in handcuffs and sentenced to four years.

The theme of covert tensions, overcome by right thinking and positive attitude, continues in the twelve-minute video entitled *You've Picked a Great Place to Work*. Here various associates testify to the "essential feeling of family for which Wal-Mart is so well-known," leading up to the conclusion that we don't need a union. Once, long ago, unions had a place in American society, but they "no longer have much to offer workers," which is why people are leaving them "by the droves." Wal-Mart is booming; unions are declining: judge for yourself. But we are warned that "unions have been targeting Wal-Mart for years." Why? For the dues money of course. Think of what you would lose with a union: first, your dues money, which could be $20 a month "and sometimes much more." Second, you would lose "your voice" because the union would insist on doing your talking for you. Finally, you might lose even your wages and benefits because they would all be "at risk on the bargaining table." You have to wonder—and I imagine some of my teenage fellow orientees may be doing so—why such fiends as these union organizers, such outright extortionists, are allowed to roam free in the land.

There is more, much more than I could ever absorb, even if it were spread out over a semester-long course.

On the reasonable assumption that none of us is planning to go home and curl up with the "Wal-Mart Associate Handbook," our trainers start reading it out loud to us, pausing every few paragraphs to ask, "Any questions?" There never are. Barry, the seventeen-year-old to my left, mutters that his "butt hurts." Sonya, the tiny African American woman across from me, seems frozen in terror. I have given up on looking perky and am fighting to keep my eyes open. No nose or other facial jewelry, we learn; earrings must be small and discreet, not dangling; no blue jeans except on Friday, and then you have to pay $1 for the privilege of wearing them. No "grazing," that is, eating from food packages that somehow become open; no "time theft." This last sends me drifting off in a sci-fi direction: *And as the time thieves headed back to the year 3420, loaded with weekends and days off looted from the twenty-first century* . . . Finally, a question. The old guy who is being hired as a people greeter wants to know, "What is time theft?" Answer: Doing anything other than working during company time, anything at all. Theft of *our* time is not, however, an issue. There are stretches amounting to many minutes when all three of our trainers wander off, leaving us to sit there in silence or take the opportunity to squirm. Or our junior trainers go through a section of the handbook, and then Roberta, returning from some other business, goes over the same section again. My eyelids droop and I consider walking out. I have seen time move more swiftly during seven-hour airline delays. At least you can read a book or get up and walk around, take a leak.

On breaks, I drink coffee purchased at the Radio Grill, as the in-house fast-food place is called, the real stuff with caffeine, more because I'm concerned about being alert for the late-night drive home than out of any need to absorb all the Wal-Mart trivia coming my way.

Now, here's a drug the drug warriors ought to take a little more interest in. Since I don't normally drink it at all—iced tea can usually be counted on for enough of a kick—the coffee has an effect like reagent-grade Dexedrine: my pulse races, my brain overheats, and the result in this instance is a kind of delirium. I find myself overly challenged by the little kindergarten-level tasks we are now given to do, such an affixing my personal bar code to my ID card, then sticking on the punchout letters to spell my name. The letters keep curling up and sticking to my fingers, so I stop at "Barb," or more precisely, "B*AR*B," drifting off to think of all the people I know who have gentrified their names in recent years—Patsy to Patricia, Dick to Richard, and so forth— while I am going in the other direction. Now we start taking turns going to the computers to begin our CBL, or Computer-Based Learning, and I become transfixed by the HIV-inspired module entitled "Bloodborne Pathogens," on what to do in the event that pools of human blood should show up on the sales floor. All right, you put warning cones around the puddles, don protective gloves, etc., but I can't stop trying to envision the circumstances in which these pools might arise: an associate uprising? a guest riot? I have gone through six modules, three more than we are supposed to do tonight—the rest are to be done in our spare moments over the next few weeks—when one of the trainers gently pries me away from the computer. We are allowed now to leave.

There follows the worst of many sleepless nights to come. On the drive home along the interstate, a guy doing over eighty passes me on the right at a few angstroms' distance, making the point that any highway has far more exits than you can see, infinitely many— final exits, that is. At this hour, which is nearly midnight, it takes me fifteen minutes to find a parking place, and another five to walk to the apartment, where I find that Budgie, distraught by my long absence, has gone totally postal. Feathers litter the floor under his cage, and he refuses to return to it even after a generous forty-five minutes of head time. I want to be fresh for my first day in plumbing tomorrow—Menards is still my choice—but a lot of small things have been going wrong, and at this level of finances, nothing wrong is ever quite small enough. My watch battery ran out and I had to spend $11 to get it replaced. My khakis developed a prominent ink stain that took three wash cycles ($3.75) and a treatment with Shout Gel ($1.29) to remove. There was the $20 application fee at the Park Plaza, plus $20 for the belt I need for Menards, purchased only after comparison shopping at a consignment store. And why hadn't I asked what that knife and tape measure are going to cost? I discover that the phone is no longer taking incoming calls or recording voice mail, so who knows what housing opportunities I have missed. Around two in the morning, I pop a Unisom to counteract the still-raging caffeine, but at five Budgie takes his revenge, greeting the prospect of dawn, which is still comfortably remote, with a series of scandalized squawks.

I am due at Menards at noon. At this point, although I have not formally accepted either job, I realize I am officially employed at both places, Wal-Mart and Menards. Maybe I'll combine both jobs or just blow off Wal-Mart and go for the better money at Menards. But Wal-Mart, with its endless orientation, has, alas, already sunk its talons into me. People working more than one job—and in effect I would be doing that for a day by going from my three-to-eleven stint at Wal-Mart to a day at Menards—have to take sleep deprivation in stride. I do not. I am shaky, my brain fried like that egg in the

Partnership for a Drug-Free America commercial. How am I going to master the science of plumbing products when I can barely summon the concentration required to assemble a breakfast of peanut butter and toast? The world is coming at me in high-contrast snapshots, deprived of narrative continuity. I call Menards and get Paul on the line to clear up what exactly my shift is supposed to be. Steve—or was it Walt?—said noon till eleven, but that would be eleven hours, right?

"Right," he says. "You want to be full-time, don't you?"

And you're going to pay me ten dollars an hour?

"Ten dollars?" Paul asks, "Who told you ten?" He'll have to check on that; it can't be right.

Now thoroughly unnerved, I tell him I'm not working an eleven-hour shift, not without time and a half after eight. I don't tell him about the generations of workers who fought and sometimes died for the ten-hour day and then the eight, although this is very much on my mind.[2] I just tell him I'm going to send my knife, my vest, and my tape measure back. In the days that follow I will try to rationalize this decision by telling myself that, given Wal-Mart's position as the nation's largest private employer, whatever I experience there will at least be of grand social significance. But this is just a way of prettifying yet another dumb mistake, the one involving all that coffee. The embarrassing truth is that I am just too exhausted to work, especially for eleven hours in a row.

---

2. Under the Fair Labor Standards Act it is in fact illegal not to pay time and a half for hours worked above forty hours a week. Certain categories of workers—professionals, managers, and farmworkers—are not covered by the FLSA, but retail workers are not among them.

Why hadn't I asked all these questions about wages and hours before? For that matter, why hadn't I bargained with Roberta when she called to tell me I'd passed the drug test—told her $7 an hour would be fine, as long as the benefits included a free lakeside condo with hot tub? At least part of the answer, which I only figured out weeks later, lies in the employers' deft handling of the hiring process. First you are an applicant, then suddenly you are an orientee. You're handed the application form and, a few days later, you're being handed the uniform and warned against nose rings and stealing. There's no intermediate point in the process in which you confront the potential employer as a free agent, entitled to cut her own deal. The intercalation of the drug test between application and hiring tilts the playing field even further, establishing that you, and not the employer, are the one who has something to prove. Even in the tightest labor market—and it doesn't get any tighter than Minneapolis, where I would probably have been welcome to apply at any commercial establishment I entered—the person who has precious labor to sell can be made to feel one down, way down, like a supplicant with her hand stretched out.

FOR DISCUSSION

1. Why does Ehrenreich say that an anthropologist might call the Wal-Mart training video an introduction to the "Cult of Sam"? (101)

2. Why does Ehrenreich point out that Wal-Mart defines "time theft" as "doing anything other than working during company time, anything at all" but that "theft" of the employees' time is not an issue? (103)

3. Why does Ehrenreich include the details of her small expenses and remark that "a lot of small things have been going wrong, and at this level of finances, nothing wrong is ever quite small enough"? (105)

4. Why does Ehrenreich only figure out "weeks later" that part of the reason she did not ask about work hours and wages during the hiring process was the lack of an "intermediate point in the process in which you confront the potential employer as a free agent"? (107)

FOR FURTHER REFLECTION

1. Does Ehrenreich's actual position as a successful journalist and author with a reputation for criticizing large corporations affect your view of her account? Do you think readers should trust Ehrenreich's account?

2. Given the situations Ehrenreich describes, what are some changes that would make the United States labor market more fair for low-wage employees?

Paco Underhill (1951–) is founding president of Envirosell, a global behavioral research and consulting firm based in New York City with branch offices around the world. He is an expert on consumer behavior and trends. His research has made important contributions to the field of consumer psychology, demonstrating how factors such as gender and anatomy encourage people to buy certain things at certain times in particular environments. Underhill is author of *Why We Buy: The Science of Shopping* (1999), published in twenty-seven languages; *Call of the Mall* (2004), a humorous walking tour of an American shopping mall, and *What Women Want* (2010). In this excerpt from *Call of the Mall*, Underhill tours a mall with his friend Carol, a visual merchandiser responsible for all aspects of product display for a major retailer.

Sex and the Mall

Now we're leaving cosmetics behind and strolling the rest of the mall. We've gone a few paces before we come upon a window display that stops us, which is what they're supposed to do.

We're looking into the window of H&M, the giant Swedish apparel chain. They've done an outstanding job of cornering the market for what I call disposable cloths—garments that look really trendy and stylish but cost around $25 or less. Teenagers worship H&M. The window is populated by sylphlike mannequins, reed-thin representations of your average postadolescent girl-woman. Not one of them is dressed in anything you'd expect to see worn at Sunday school.

"My niece will *make* my sister take her to H&M every time they visit me in New York," Carol says. "My sister likes the prices but hates the styles."

"Some of it's like hooker wear, isn't it?"

"Teenage hooker wear."

"Older people look at how girls dress, with the belly exposed and hipbones exposed and the tight, flimsy tops and skin-tight pants, and it alarms them. But young girls have no idea what a hooker looks like or even what a hooker *is*. To her, it's just how glamorous young women look today."

"The other thing to keep in mind is that grandmothers today also dress less conservatively than ever before. When the line moves, it moves for everybody."

We move a few stores along, until the window with the number-one "capture rate" in any mall in America stops us again.

"Here's where mall sex really started," Carol says.

"Is that what Victoria's Secret is selling?"

"I think it's selling sex *appeal*. Inexpensive sex appeal. Women visit this store to get in touch with their feminine side. The company has taken underwear from being a staple to being something where there's a personal connection. This is especially true for women thirty-five and younger. Though I always wonder what the woman who's over thirty-five is supposed to do about getting in touch with *her* feminine side.

"Another example of how the mall reflects real life— because when women hit a certain age, society stops thinking of them as sexy. The stores are an example of that. Compare the H&M window with a window aimed at the fifty-year-old woman."

"Susan Sarandon must be pushing fifty-five."

"Sophia Loren passed sixty many moons ago. Where do you think she shops?"

"The funny part is that while Victoria's Secret sells modestly priced goods, older women could and absolutely *would* pay a good deal more for lingerie," I point out. "They're the ones who have the higher disposable income, and their tastes are more sophisticated. They're ready to splurge a little on themselves, to go along with the pedicures, facials, body waxing, spa treatments, and botox. They'd pay big bucks for gorgeous. high-quality underwear. If only somebody would sell it to them."

"There *are* fancier brands of lingerie, but sold either in department stores or in boutiques. Victoria's Secret has a special label for older shoppers, but I think the company is missing a bet by not opening a separate chain of stores for them. They could call it Victoria's Mother's Secret."

"They're also not aggressively serving the plus-size woman of *any* age," I say. "Now, maybe they don't want older or bigger women because they're afraid it would drive away the young, thin shopper. But it seems there must be a way for them to go after those other markets, too."

"Especially when you consider that a substantial percentage of the population of American women is overweight," says Carol. "And they're not even all old. I see a lot of fat teenagers and women in their twenties."

"Well, there *is* a high fashion chain now for young chubbies."

"I've seen it. There's a chain of stores called Torrid. And the clothes they sell are *sexy*."

"Yes indeed. Big young girls tend to get big in the right places."

"And they're not bashful, either. As long as they're fat and curvy, they can make it work. Major cleavage. Narrow at the waist and tight on the butt."

"This is one of those weird gulfs between media imagery and real life," I say. "Judging by the fashion magazines you'd think that women would be ashamed to be overweight. Judging by how the weight of the average American girl has gone up, though, you get the opposite impression. But even if Victoria's Secret carried big sizes, could big girls get away with wearing this stuff?"

"Like thongs, you mean?"

"Well, yeah."

"Big girls wear thongs, believe me," Carol says. "And they buy them here, too. You won't see plus-size mannequins, but thong sizes absolutely go up to extra-large, you'll notice."

"Victoria's Secret really *did* make it okay for the average young woman to wear racy underwear."

"Yes," says Carol, "and the advantage of the low prices is that you can wear the stuff as long as it's fun, then replace it. This is where girls go when they first begin buying their own underwear. This is how they announce, 'My mom doesn't buy my underwear anymore.' Victoria's Secret sells hottie underwear for Catholic girls. It's not sleazy or even too sophisticated. They steered clear of the Frederick's of Hollywood image of a lingerie store. They got rid of the red and made it all pink."

"So, they do a good job, right?" I ask.

"They could do better." Carol says. "One problem I have with *all* lingerie stores is that—look, here you have a section of bras. And nowadays, every bra does something a little different. It's gotten to be like cosmetics in that regard. But there's no way to know which bra does what unless you've had personal experience with it. There's no information here to explain that this bra does blah, blah, and blah. This one pushes them together, and this one shoves them up, and here's one for strapless dresses. Now, partly that is intentional. They don't want you to get too much information on your own. They'd rather even confuse you a little so that you'll take a whole bunch of bras into the dressing room, because the more you take in, they know, the better the chance that you'll buy multiple items. They've measured this, and they're right. But at the same time, it frustrates consumers."

Carol is right about that: There's no communication here, no sign that says, for example, "If you've always loved this kind of bra, you'll probably love this new style, too." Maybe there could even be an informational display telling a young woman how to build a proper lingerie wardrobe. Like, you'll need one of these and two of those and here's how to choose these little thingies.

"Women pick up their knowledge of cosmetics and lingerie in a totally ad hoc way," Carol says. "You see something about push-up bras in a magazine, or your older sister lends you her new lip gloss, and you kind of piece your information together like that."

"'It's like locker room conversation."

"Right. You see somebody else try it, and you ask a few questions . . ."

"The same way adolescents learn about sex. You read three issues of *Cosmo*, and then a fifteen-year-old tells you the rest."

We've made it all the way up to the second level of the mall. We've broken out of that little cluster of stores serving young female sexuality. But we're now looking into a den of older female sexuality—the threshold of a fancy department store's fragrance section. Department stores always put the fragrance section at the entrance.

"Is this positioning a good idea or bad, do you think?" I ask.

"Bad. The thing about fine fragrance is that people buy it twice a year."

"Christmas . . ."

". . . and Mother's Day. Maybe Valentines Day, too, although men are much less confident buying perfume than women are."

"Tell me what you think of that," I say, nodding toward the huge poster above the counter. It shows a brooding, sulky-lipped hunk, a stud of maybe twenty-one or so, with hairless, highly sculpted pectoral muscles on prominent display.

"It doesn't do anything for me," Carol says. "He's the son of the consumer, not the man she's going to bed with. I bet he's a good fifteen years younger than the average shopper in this section. I mean, put Harrison Ford up there, not this twenty-year-old. He's a *boy*.

This is the Madison Avenue mentality at work. Some creatives and executives in an ad agency dream this up and cast it and style it and shoot it without bothering to understand the consumer—the person who will have to look at it. They imagine how the picture will look in the ad in *Vanity Fair* or on TV, without considering how it will play in the store. They may want to target a younger consumer. They feel that the way to do this is with a new men's fragrance geared toward this beautiful young man. They hope they'll bring a younger woman to the counter to buy this new fragrance for her young man, and then she'll shop the cosmetics. too."

"Won't that work?"

"Look around."

Ouch. Department stores' core shoppers *are* getting old, and no young women are taking their place.

"Also, men anywhere near fragrance or cosmetics is a nonstarter."

"Same for lingerie?" I ask.

"Nearly as bad."

"Apparel?"

"About the same."

"If a man is uncomfortable hanging around in the perfume aisle or shopping the racks of undergarments, is he likely to buy there?" I ask.

"I don't see how he could."

"I wonder what would happen if, say, Victoria's Secret were to open a ministore just for male shoppers at Christmas or Valentine's Day. It might look a lot like the store now does. But it would work differently," I say. "It would have to actually address size and function, and in a completely new way. Women know their sizes, and so its no great trick to handle that when they're shopping for themselves."

"A woman knows her man's sizes, but men don't know women's, do they?"

"Men don't even know their *own* sizes," I say. "Remember, we saw men's underwear being sold to women in Filene's. Can you imagine finding women's underwear for sale in a men's clothing store? Years ago, one of our video cameras caught a guy shopping the underwear rack when he suddenly twisted around, pulled out his waistband in back and attempted to read the size on the label. It's conceivable that in his entire life he had never before bought his own underwear—first his mother bought it, then his girlfriends, now his wife."

"Can you imagine a woman not knowing what size panties she wears?" Carol says.

"Unimaginable."

"Anyway, you can see how men might feel ill at ease buying lingerie for women. For starters, he doesn't know her size. I guess if he was really intent on buying her something intimate, he could always snoop around in her dresser drawer and read a few labels."

"True," I say, "but that requires some forethought. Plus, it sounds perverted. If he gets caught, she may think he's looking for something lacy to wear under his Dockers. How would you handle ladies' lingerie for the impulse gift buy? It's February 13, and he's in a panic. He's already been to the jewelry store and didn't find anything he liked in his price range. He's prowling the mall like a desperate animal. Time is running out. Suddenly he notices a display window filled with lingerie. The lightbulb goes on—for what a modest piece of jewelry costs, he can get something truly extravagant in the fancy underwear department."

"If only he knew her size," Carol says. "It's tragic."

"What do you suggest?"

"He can say to the saleswoman, "She's around your height . . .""

"Or, 'Gee, I think her breasts are a little bigger than yours.'"

"Or, 'Hmm, let me hold your butt a second so I can figure out if she's a medium or a large.'"

"That might be beyond what most salesclerks are willing to abide, even those working on commission," I say.

"How about if they had mannequins of various sizes?"

"And a bunch of male customers lined up, fondling them? I don't see that, either. Maybe a gift certificate works best here."

"Or maybe at gift time the window display is dominated by garments where size is easiest—robes instead of bras."

"Anything sheer," I say.

"Or black leather," Carol says.

"The point is that it's possible to make women's merchandise easier for men to buy. And that doing so around the romance-friendly holidays might not be a bad idea. I think if men walked by Victoria's Secret and saw that some of the signs and posters and photographs were directed specifically at them, they'd feel more welcome. Just something that says, 'Sir, we'd love to show you a few perfect gifts for her.' Because right now that entire store announces, 'Hey, buddy, stay the hell out of here.'"

"It's true," she says. "You don't see many men in there, do you?"

"Sure don't. And the few who are here are all just tagging along with wives or girlfriends, with their eyes cast downward in case they accidentally see something. They're ashamed! Look at that one pathetic little chair in front of the pillar, up by the register. That's the entire accommodation for men who end up inside the store. It looks like a punishment—like the dunce chair. Merely by sitting there, a man announces, 'I am an emasculated husband waiting uncomfortably for my wife to find a thong in her size.' Especially in a mall store, where you know the woman is likely to be with her family, you've got to plan for the nonshopper as much as the shopper. A Victoria's Secret on a city street, where the typical customer is a woman on her lunch break, can get away with neglecting the needs of men and children. A mall store cannot."

"But this mall does have areas where people who aren't shopping can just sit and wait or read the paper or watch everybody else, doesn't it?" Carol says.

"Sure it does. But think about the way it works in real life. The couple is walking along when suddenly it hits her that she needs underwear. Here are her choices. She can ask him to come inside the store with her. Or, she can run in alone and leave him standing out here cooling his heels in front of a window populated by panties and bras, which means that every window shopper who passes will be staring straight at him, too. He'll love that. Or, he can find another store to go and browse, assuming there's anything he finds remotely interesting in the immediate vicinity. Maybe there is a record store or bookstore or the new Apple computer store or something like that. But most malls now group merchandise categories, meaning the women's clothing store is probably surrounded by other shops of interest to women. So he's screwed. He could go all the way down the corridor and around the corner to the public seating area. But he may not even know it's there, and secondly, she's assured him she'll just be two minutes, and so he's got to ask himself if it's worth his while to go so far to kill a hundred and twenty seconds. If there was a small waiting area just outside the store, he'd probably go there. But then you run the risk that you'll have a gaggle of guys loitering outside the lingerie store, which isn't the most agreeable setting for female push-up bra shoppers. I think that lingerie stores should do more to make males feel at ease."

"I disagree completely," Carol says. "No woman in her right mind wants to come into this store with her husband and children. This is not the kind of thing you want to be shopping for where your guy or, even worse, your eight-year-old son, can watch. You're in here to create a little romantic fantasy starring yourself, and it doesn't involve somebody's lumpy husband or bratty kids whining to go to the food court. I think it's smart of them to make it difficult for men to loiter in here, and I bet they did it as a conscious decision."

That's a good point. It runs completely counter to all that we've learned about the science of shopping, and yet I am convinced that maybe she's on to something. We once studied a store that sold dishes and tabletops and so on. We saw that many women came in with their husbands, but the men got bored tagging along, and, as a result, the women seemed pressured. The store tried adding products men might browse—bar items like cocktail shakers, shot glasses, and so on. When that happened, the men went off on their own, and total shopping time for couples rose. Sales rose, too.

But perhaps what's right for dishes is totally *wrong* for lingerie. Maybe the woman wants to tell her husband and kids to get lost for fifteen minutes, and going into Victoria's Secret is a good way to do so.

A recent study of how men and women differ when it comes to the mall turned up this fact: Men, once you get them in the door, are much more interested in the social aspect of malls than the shopping part, whereas women say the social aspect is important but shopping comes first. Men enjoy the mall as a form of recreation—they like watching people and browsing around in stores more than shopping. Maybe they'll spend fifteen minutes in a bookstore or a stereo store and leave without buying a thing. They treat it like an information-gathering trip. Men also like the nonretail parts—the rock-climbing walls, the food courts, anything that doesn't actually require them to enter stores and look at, try on, or buy merchandise. Women, of course, are there for *exactly* those things. The only females who truly love the nonshopping aspects of the mall are teenage girls. They love shopping, of course, but they also love the food courts and video arcade and all that stuff, too. And that's probably because the mall is the only nonhome, nonschool environment they have. But they outgrow that by the time they're in college. From then on, they're at malls to shop.

"Let's get back to where to put fragrance if we want men to buy it," I say.

"In Sears near the power tools?"

"I bet more men would buy it there than in the cosmetics department "

"Where else?"

"Closer to jewelry might work," I say. "In fact, you could group all the traditional gifts that men give women and see how that works. That's one of the few remaining advantages this department store has over a specialty shop or boutique—that wide range of merchandise. They can set a little creative with their juxtapositions."

"So you'd have fragrance, jewelry, and lingerie all together in a way that feels male-accessible," Carol says.

"Yeah. You'd put up graphics showing a man making a purchase of something gift-wrapped with a pink bow. With that big hint, at least some men might be psychologically able to enter the area and shop it. Put a salesclerk at the entrance to guide men across the threshold—a good-looking woman to take him by the arm and gently drag him inside. And I think women would be willing to buy things there, too."

"The Extravagance Shop."

"Right. I'd give it a name to appeal to guys. It would give them permission to shop there, something men really don't have now in women's departments. And I'd make sure it was marketed to male shoppers, especially around the usual gift times like Christmas, Valentine's Day. . . ."

"Yes," says Carol. "Because fragrance only gets shopped twice a year, having it at the entrance gives the impression that the store is empty."

"It is less crowded there than anywhere else, but is that a bad thing?'

"Sure, who wants to shop at a store where nobody goes? It's like going into an empty restaurant. It doesn't inspire great confidence."

"Do you know why fragrance is traditionally right inside the entrance in department stores?" I say. "Because, back in the days before cars, the perfume section was a bulwark against the stench of horse manure coming in from the street."

"Fascinating," says Carol.

Sounds like Carol's had her fill of the mall, considering that today's her day off and she spends plenty of work time in shopping centers anyway. It's an occupational hazard, mall-sickness, one even I've experienced. Time to move on.

FOR DISCUSSION

1. Why does Underhill structure this chapter as an extended conversation with a female companion, as they walk through the mall? What is the effect of presenting information about the mall in this way rather than in the form of a traditional essay?

2. How is Carol distinguishing between "sex" and "sex appeal" when she says that Victoria's Secret is selling sex appeal?

3. Why do Underhill and his companion disagree about whether it would be a good idea for the lingerie store to create a comfortable waiting area for men? Whose point of view is most convincing?

4. What is Underhill's attitude toward the merchandising efforts he describes?

FOR FURTHER REFLECTION

1. Why might it be that "department stores' core shoppers *are* getting old, and no young women are taking their place"? (116)

2. When you go to a mall or department store, how strongly do store design, merchandise displays, and other marketing techniques influence your decisions about what to buy?

Amy Tan (1952–), was born in Oakland, California, the daughter of Chinese immigrants. Before she began writing fiction, she studied English and linguistics, earning a bachelor's and a master's degree from San Jose State University in California, and she worked as a technical writer. She is the author of *The Joy Luck Club* (1989), a novel that won numerous awards. The novel explores the cultural and generational struggles between Chinese American daughters and their mothers. Her other novels include *The Kitchen God's Wife* (1991), *The Hundred Secret Senses* (1995), *The Bonesetter's Daughter* (2001), and *Saving Fish from Drowning* (2005). She has also written children's books and collaborated on the screenplay of *The Joy Luck Club*, which was made into a film directed by Wayne Wang in 1993. In the following excerpt from *The Joy Luck Club*, Jing-mei Woo assumes her mother's place at the Joy Luck Club's mahjong table, shortly after her mother's death.

The Joy Luck Club
(selection)

When I arrived at the Hsus' house, where the Joy Luck Club is meeting tonight, the first person I see is my father. "There she is! Never on time!" he announces. And it's true. Everybody's already here, seven family friends in their sixties and seventies. They look up and laugh at me, always tardy, a child still at thirty-six.

I'm shaking, trying to hold something inside. The last time I saw them, at the funeral, I had broken down and cried big gulping sobs. They must wonder now how someone like me can take my mother's place. A friend once told me that my mother and I were alike, that we had the same wispy hand gestures, the same girlish laugh and sideways look. When I shyly told my mother this, she seemed insulted and said, "You don't even know little percent of me! How can you be me?" And she's right. How can I be my mother at Joy Luck?

"Auntie, Uncle," I say repeatedly, nodding to each person there. I have always called these old family friends Auntie and Uncle. And then I walk over and stand next to my father.

He's looking at the Jongs' pictures of their recent China trip. "Look at that," he says politely, pointing to a photo of the Jongs' tour group standing on wide slab steps. There is nothing in this picture that shows it was taken in China rather than San Francisco, or any other city for that matter. But my father doesn't seem to be looking at the picture anyway. It's as though everything were the same to him, nothing stands out. He has always

125

been politely indifferent. But what's the Chinese word that means indifferent because you can't *see* any differences? That's how troubled I think he is by my mother's death.

"Will you look at that," he says, pointing to another nondescript picture.

The Hsus' house feels heavy with greasy odors. Too many Chinese meals cooked in a too small kitchen, too many once fragrant smells compressed into a thin layer of invisible grease. I remember how my mother used to go into other people's houses and restaurants and wrinkle her nose, then whisper very loudly: "I can see and feel the stickiness with my nose."

I have not been to the Hsus' house in many years, but the living room is exactly the same as I remember it. When Auntie An-mei and Uncle George moved to the Sunset district from Chinatown twenty-five years ago, they bought new furniture. It's all there, still looking mostly new under yellowed plastic. The same turquoise couch shaped in a semicircle of nubby tweed. The colonial end tables made out of heavy maple. A lamp of fake cracked porcelain. Only the scroll-length calendar, free from the Bank of Canton, changes every year.

I remember this stuff, because when we were children, Auntie An-mei didn't let us touch any of her new furniture except through the clear plastic coverings. On Joy Luck nights, my parents brought me to the Hsus'. Since I was the guest, I had to take care of all the younger children, so many children it seemed as if there were always one baby who was crying from having bumped its head on a table leg.

"You are responsible," said my mother, which meant I was in trouble if anything was spilled, burned, lost, broken, or dirty. I was responsible, no matter who did it. She and Auntie An-mei were dressed up in funny Chinese dresses with stiff stand-up collars and blooming branches of embroidered silk sewn over their breasts. These clothes were too fancy for real Chinese people, I thought, and too strange for American parties. In those days, before my mother told me her Kweilin story, I imagined Joy Luck was a shameful Chinese custom, like the secret gathering of the Ku Klux Klan or the tom-tom dances of TV Indians preparing for war.

But tonight, there's no mystery. The Joy Luck aunties are all wearing slacks, bright print blouses, and different versions of sturdy walking shoes. We are all seated around the dining room table under a lamp that looks like a Spanish candelabra. Uncle George puts on his bifocals and starts the meeting by reading the minutes:

"Our capital account is $24,825, or about $6,206 a couple, $3,103 per person. We sold Subaru for a loss at six and three-quarters. We bought a hundred shares of Smith International at seven. Our thanks to Lindo and Tin Jong for the goodies. The red bean soup was especially delicious. The March meeting had to be canceled until further notice. We were sorry to have to bid a fond farewell to our dear friend Suyuan and extended our sympathy to the Canning Woo family. Respectfully submitted, George Hsu, president and secretary."

That's it. I keep thinking the others will start talking about my mother, the wonderful friendship they shared, and why I am here in her spirit, to be the fourth corner and carry on the idea my mother came up with on a hot day in Kweilin.

But everybody just nods to approve the minutes. Even my father's head bobs up and down routinely. And it seems to me my mother's life has been shelved for new business.

Auntie An-mei heaves herself up from the table and moves slowly to the kitchen to prepare the food. And Auntie Lin, my mother's best friend, moves to the turquoise sofa, crosses her arms, and watches the men still seated at the table. Auntie Ying, who seems to shrink even more every time I see her, reaches into her knitting bag and pulls out the start of a tiny blue sweater.

The Joy Luck uncles begin to talk about stocks they are interested in buying. Uncle Jack, who is Auntie Ying's younger brother, is very keen on a company that mines gold in Canada.

"It's a great hedge on inflation," he says with authority. He speaks the best English, almost accentless. I think my mother's English was the worst, but she always thought her Chinese was the best. She spoke Mandarin slightly blurred with a Shanghai dialect.

"Weren't we going to play mahjong tonight?" I whisper loudly to Auntie Ying, who's slightly deaf.

"Later," she says, "after midnight."

"Ladies, are you at this meeting or not?" says Uncle George.

After everybody votes unanimously for the Canada gold stock, I go into the kitchen to ask Auntie An-mei why the Joy Luck Club started investing in stocks.

"We used to play mahjong, winner take all. But the same people were always winning, the same people always losing," she says. She is stuffing wonton, one chopstick jab of gingery meat dabbed onto a thin skin and then a single fluid turn with her hand that seals the skin into the shape of a tiny nurse's cap. "You can't have luck when someone else has skill. So long time ago, we decided to invest in the stock market. There's no skill in that. Even your mother agreed."

Auntie An-mei takes count of the tray in front of her. She's already made five rows of eight wonton each.

"Forty wonton, eight people, ten each, five row more," she says aloud to herself, and then continues stuffing. "We got smart. Now we can all win and lose equally. We can have stock market luck. And we can play mahjong for fun, just for a few dollars, winner take all. Losers take home leftovers! So everyone can have some joy. Smart-hanh?"

I watch Auntie An-mei make more wonton. She has quick, expert fingers. She doesn't have to think about what she is doing. That's what my mother used to complain about, that Auntie An-mei never thought about what she was doing.

"She's not stupid," said my mother on one occasion, "but she has no spine. Last week, I had a good idea for her. I said to her, Let's go to the consulate and ask for papers for your brother. And she almost wanted to drop her things and go right then. But later she talked to someone. Who knows who? And that person told her she can get her brother in bad trouble in China. That person said FBI will put her on a list and give her trouble in the U.S. the rest of her life. That person said, You ask for a house loan and they say no loan, because your brother is a communist. I said, You already have a house! But still she was scared.

"Aunti An-mei runs this way and that," said my mother, "and she doesn't know why."

As I watch Auntie An-mei, I see a short bent woman in her seventies, with a heavy bosom and thin, shapeless legs. She has the flattened soft fingertips of an old woman. I wonder what Auntie An-mei did to inspire a lifelong stream of criticism from my mother. Then again, it seemed my mother was always displeased with all her friends, with me, and even with my father. Something was always missing. Something always needed improving. Something was not in balance. This one or that had too much of one element, not enough of another.

The elements were from my mother's own version of organic chemistry. Each person is made of five elements, she told me.

Too much fire and you had a bad temper. That was like my father, whom my mother always criticized for his cigarette habit and who always shouted back that she should keep her thoughts to herself. I think he now feels guilty that he didn't let my mother speak her mind.

Too little wood and you bent too quickly to listen to other people's ideas, unable to stand on your own. This was like my Auntie An-mei.

Too much water and you flowed in too many directions, like myself, for having started half a degree in biology, then half a degree in art, and then finishing neither when I went off to work for a small ad agency as a secretary, later becoming a copywriter.

I used to dismiss her criticisms as just more of her Chinese superstitions, beliefs that conveniently fit the circumstances. In my twenties, while taking Introduction to Psychology, I tried to tell her why she shouldn't criticize so much, why it didn't lead to a healthy learning environment.

"There's a school of thought," I said, "that parents shouldn't criticize children. They should encourage instead. You know, people rise to other people's expectations. And when you criticize, it just means you're expecting failure."

"That's the trouble," my mother said. "You never rise. Lazy to get up. Lazy to rise to expectations."

"Time to eat," Auntie An-mei happily announces, bringing out a steaming pot of the wonton she was just wrapping. There are piles of food on the table, served buffet style, just like at the Kweilin feasts. My father is digging into the chow mein, which still sits in an over-size aluminum pan surrounded by little plastic packets of soy sauce. Auntie An-mei must have bought this on Clement Street. The wonton soup smells wonderful with delicate sprigs of cilantro floating on top. I'm drawn first to a large platter of *chaswei*, sweet barbecued pork cut into coin-sized slices, and then to a whole assortment of what I've always called finger goodies—thin-skinned pastries filled with chopped pork, beef, shrimp, and unknown stuffings that my mother used to describe as "nutritious things."

Eating is not a gracious event here. It's as though everybody had been starving. They push large forkfuls into their mouths, jab at more pieces of pork, one right after the other. They are not like the ladies of Kweilin, who I always imagined savored their food with a certain detached delicacy.

And then, almost as quickly as they started, the men get up and leave the table. As if on cue, the women peck at last morsels and then carry plates and bowls to the kitchen and dump them in the sink. The women take turns washing their hands, scrubbing them vigorously. Who started this ritual? I too put my plate in the sink and wash my hands. The women are talking about the Jongs' China trip, then they move toward a room in the back of the apartment. We pass another room, what used to be the bedroom shared by the four Hsu sons. The bunk beds with their scuffed, splintery ladders are still there. The Joy Luck uncles are already seated at the card table. Uncle George is dealing out cards, fast, as though he learned this technique in a casino. My father is passing out Pall Mall cigarettes, with one already dangling from his lips.

And then we get to the room in the back, which was once shared by the three Hsu girls. We were all childhood friends. And now they've all grown and married and I'm here to play in their room again. Except for the smell of camphor, it feels the same—as if Rose, Ruth, and Janice might soon walk in with their hair rolled up in big orange-juice cans and plop down on their identical narrow beds. The white chenille bedspreads are so worn they are almost translucent. Rose and I used to pluck the nubs out while talking about our boy problems. Everything is the same, except now a mahogany-colored mahjong table sits in the center. And next to it is a floor lamp, a long black pole with three oval spotlights attached like the broad leaves of a rubber plant.

Nobody says to me, "Sit here, this is where your mother used to sit." But I can tell even before everyone sits down. The chair closest to the door has an emptiness to it. But the feeling doesn't really have to do with the chair. It's her place on the table. Without having anyone tell me, I know her corner on the table was the East.

The East is where things begin, my mother once told me, the direction from which the sun rises, where the wind comes from.

Auntie An-mei, who is sitting on my left, spills the tiles onto the green felt tabletop and then says to me, "Now we wash tiles." We swirl them with our hands in a circular motion. They make a cool swishing sound as they bump into one another.

"Do you win like your mother?" asks Auntie Lin across from me. She is not smiling.

"I only played a little in college with some Jewish friends."

"Annh! Jewish mahjong," she says in disgusted tones. "Not the same thing." This is what my mother used to say, although she could never explain exactly why.

"Maybe I shouldn't play tonight. I'll just watch," I offer.

Auntie Lin looks exasperated, as though I were a simple child: "How can we play with just three people? Like a table with three legs, no balance. When Auntie Ying's husband died, she asked her brother to join. Your father asked you. So it's decided."

"What's the difference between Jewish and Chinese mahjong?" I once asked my mother. I couldn't tell by her answer if the games were different or just her attitude toward Chinese and Jewish people.

"Entirely different kind of playing," she said in her English explanation voice. "Jewish mahjong, they watch only for their own tile, play only with their eyes."

Then she switched to Chinese: "Chinese mahjong, you must play using your head, very tricky. You must watch what everybody else throws away and keep that in your head as well. And if nobody plays well, then the game becomes like Jewish mahjong. Why play? There's no strategy. You're just watching people make mistakes."

These kinds of explanations made me feel my mother and I spoke two different languages, which we did. I talked to her in English, she answered back in Chinese.

"So what's the difference between Chinese and Jewish mahjong?" I ask Auntie Lin.

"Aii-ya," she exclaims in a mock scolding voice. "Your mother did not teach you anything?"

Auntie Ying pats my hand. "You a smart girl. You watch us, do the same. Help us stack the tiles and make four walls."

I follow Auntie Ying, but mostly I watch Auntie Lin. She is the fastest, which means I can almost keep up with the others by watching what she does first. Auntie Ying throws the dice and I'm told that Auntie Lin has become the East wind. I've become the North wind, the last hand to play. Auntie Ying is the South and Auntie An-mei is the West. And then we start taking tiles, throwing the dice, counting back on the wall to the right number of spots where our chosen tiles lie. I re-arrange my tiles, sequences of bamboo and balls, doubles of colored number tiles, odd tiles that do not fit anywhere.

"Your mother was the best, like a pro," says Auntie An-mei while slowly sorting her tiles, considering each piece carefully.

Now we begin to play, looking at our hands, casting tiles, picking up others at an easy, comfortable pace. The Joy Luck aunties begin to make small talk, not really listening to each other. They speak in their special language, half in broken English, half in their own Chinese dialect. Auntie Ying mentions she bought yarn at half price, somewhere out in the avenues. Auntie An-mei brags about a sweater she made for her daughter Ruth's new baby. "She thought it was store-bought," she says proudly.

Auntie Lin explains how mad she got at a store clerk who refused to let her return a skirt with a broken zipper. "I was *chiszle*," she says, still fuming, "mad to death."

"But Lindo, you are still with us. You didn't die," teases Auntie Ying, and then as she laughs Auntie Lin says "*Pung!*" and "*Mahjong!*" and then spreads her tiles out, laughing back at Auntie Ying while counting up her points. We start washing tiles again and it grows quiet. I'm getting bored and sleepy.

"Oh, I have a story," says Auntie Ying loudly, startling everybody. Auntie Ying has always been the weird auntie, someone lost in her own world. My mother used to say, "Auntie Ying is not hard of hearing. She is hard of listening."

"Police arrested Mrs. Emerson's son last weekend," Auntie Ying says in a way that sounds as if she were proud to be the first with this big news. "Mrs. Chan told me at church. Too many TV set found in his car."

Auntie Lin quickly says, "Aii-ya, Mrs. Emerson good lady," meaning Mrs. Emerson didn't deserve such a terrible son. But now I see this is also said for the benefit of Auntie An-mei, whose own youngest son was arrested two years ago for selling stolen car stereos. Auntie An-mei is rubbing her tile carefully before discarding it. She looks pained.

"Everybody has TVs in China now," says Auntie Lin, changing the subject. "Our family there all has TV sets—not just black-and-white, but color and remote! They have everything. So when we asked them what we should buy them, they said nothing, it was enough that we would come to visit them. But we bought them different things anyway, VCR and Sony Walkman for the kids. They said. No, don't give it to us, but I think they liked it."

Poor Auntie An-mei rubs her tiles ever harder. I remember my mother telling me about the Hsus' trip to China three years ago. Auntie An-mei had saved two thousand dollars, all to spend on her brother's family. She had shown my mother the insides of her heavy suitcases. One was crammed with See's Nuts & Chews, M&M's, candy-coated cashews, instant hot chocolate with miniature marshmallows. My mother told me the other bag contained the most ridiculous clothes, all new: bright California-style beachwear, baseball caps, cotton pants with elastic waists, bomber jackets, Stanford sweatshirts, crew socks.

My mother had told her, "Who wants those useless things? They just want money." But Auntie An-mei said her brother was so poor and they were so rich by comparison. So she ignored my mother's advice and took the heavy bags and their two thousand dollars to China.

And when their China tour finally arrived in Hangzhou, the whole family from Ningbo was there to meet them. It wasn't just Auntie An-mei's little brother, but also his wife's stepbrothers and stepsisters, and a distant cousin, and that cousin's husband and that husband's uncle. They had all brought their mothers-in-law and children, and even their village friends who were not lucky enough to have overseas Chinese relatives to show off.

As my mother told it, "Auntie An-mei had cried before she left for China, thinking she would make her brother very rich and happy by communist standards. But when she got home, she cried to me that everyone had a palm out and she was the only one who left with an empty hand."

My mother confirmed her suspicions. Nobody wanted the sweatshirts, those useless clothes. The M&M's were thrown in the air, gone. And when the suitcases were emptied, the relatives asked what else the Hsus had brought.

Auntie An-mei and Uncle George were shaken down, not just for two thousand dollars' worth of TVs and refrigerators but also for a night's lodging for twenty-six people in the Overlooking the Lake Hotel, for three banquet tables at a restaurant that catered to rich foreigners, for three special gifts for each relative, and finally, for a loan of five thousand yuan in foreign exchange to a cousin's so-called uncle who wanted to buy a motorcycle but who later disappeared for good along with the money. When the train pulled out of Hangzhou the next day, the Hsus found themselves depleted of some nine thousand dollars' worth of goodwill. Months later, after an inspiring Christmastime service at the First Chinese Baptist Church, Auntie An-mei tried to recoup her loss by saying it truly was more blessed to give than to receive, and my mother agreed, her longtime friend had blessings for at least several lifetimes.

Listening now to Auntie Lin bragging about the virtues of her family in China, I realize that Auntie Lin is oblivious to Auntie An-mei's pain. Is Auntie Lin being mean, or is it that my mother never told anybody but me the shameful story of Auntie An-mei's greedy family?

"So, Jing-mei, you go to school now?" says Auntie Lin.

"Her name is June. They all go by their American names," says Auntie Ying.

"That's okay," I say, and I really mean it. In fact, it's even becoming fashionable for American-born Chinese to use their Chinese names.

"I'm not in school anymore, though," I say. "That was more than ten years ago."

Auntie Lin's eyebrows arch. "Maybe I'm thinking of someone else daughter," she says, but I know right away she's lying. I know my mother probably told her I was going back to school to finish my degree, because somewhere back, maybe just six months ago, we were again having this argument about my being a failure, a "college drop-off," about my going back to finish.

Once again I had told my mother what she wanted to hear: "You're right. I'll look into it."

I had always assumed we had an unspoken understanding about these things: that she didn't really mean I was a failure, and I really meant I would try to respect her opinions more. But listening to Auntie Lin tonight reminds me once again: My mother and I never really understood one another. We translated each other's meanings and I seemed to hear less than what was said, while my mother heard more. No doubt she told Auntie Lin I was going back to school to get a doctorate.

Auntie Lin and my mother were both best friends and arch enemies who spent a lifetime comparing their children. I was one month older than Waverly Jong, Auntie Lin's prized daughter. From the time we were babies, our mothers compared the creases in our belly buttons, how shapely our earlobes were, how fast we healed when we scraped our knees, how thick and dark our hair, how many shoes we wore out in one year, and later, how smart Waverly was at playing chess, how many trophies she had won last month, how many newspapers had printed her name, how many cities she had visited.

I know my mother resented listening to Auntie Lin talk about Waverly when she had nothing to come back with. At first my mother tried to cultivate some hidden genius in me. She did housework for an old retired piano teacher down the hall who gave me lessons and free use of a piano to practice on in exchange. When I failed to become a concert pianist, or even an accompanist for the church youth choir, she finally explained that I was late-blooming, like Einstein, who everyone thought was retarded until he discovered a bomb.

Now it is Auntie Ying who wins this hand of mahjong, so we count points and begin again.

"Did you know Lena move to Woodside?" asks Auntie Ying with obvious pride, looking down at the tiles, talking to no one in particular. She quickly erases her smile and tries for some modesty. "Of course, it's not best house in neighborhood, not million-dollar house, not yet. But it's good investment. Better than paying rent. Better than somebody putting you under their thumb to rub you out."

So now I know Auntie Ying's daughter, Lena, told her about my being evicted from my apartment on lower Russian Hill. Even though Lena and I are still friends, we have grown naturally cautious about telling each other too much. Still, what little we say to one another often comes back in another guise. It's the same old game, everybody talking in circles.

"It's getting late," I say after we finish the round. I start to stand up, but Auntie Lin pushes me back down into the chair.

"Stay, stay. We talk awhile, get to know you again," she says. "Been a long time."

I know this is a polite gesture on the Joy Luck aunties' part—a protest when actually they are just as eager to see me go as I am to leave. "No, I really must go now, thank you, thank you," I say, glad I remembered how the pretense goes.

"But you must stay! We have something important to tell you, from your mother," Auntie Ying blurts out in her too-loud voice. The others look uncomfortable, as if this were not how they intended to break some sort of bad news to me.

I sit down. Auntie An-mei leaves the room quickly and returns with a bowl of peanuts, then quietly shuts the door. Everybody is quiet, as if nobody knew where to begin.

It is Auntie Ying who finally speaks. "I think your mother die with an important thought on her mind," she says in halting English. And then she begins to speak in Chinese, calmly, softly.

"Your mother was a very strong woman, a good mother. She loved you very much, more than her own life. And that's why you can understand why a mother like this could never forget her other daughters. She knew they were alive, and before she died she wanted to find her daughters in China."

The babies in Kweilin, I think. I was not those babies. The babies in a sling on her shoulder. Her other daughters. And now I feel as if I were in Kweilin amidst the bombing and I can see these babies lying on the side of the road, their red thumbs popped out of their mouths, screaming to be reclaimed. Somebody took them away. They're safe. And now my mother's left me forever, gone back to China to get these babies. I can barely hear Auntie Ying's voice.

"She had searched for years, written letters back and forth," says Auntie Ying. "And last year she got an address. She was going to tell your father soon. Aii-ya, what a shame. A lifetime of waiting."

Auntie An-mei interrupts with an excited voice: "So your aunties and I, we wrote to this address," she says. "We say that a certain party, your mother, want to meet another certain party. And this party write back to us. They are your sisters, Jing-mei."

My sisters, I repeat to myself, saying these two words together for the first time.

Auntie An-mei is holding a sheet of paper as thin as wrapping tissue. In perfectly straight vertical rows I see Chinese characters written in blue fountain-pen ink. A word is smudged. A tear? I take the letter with shaking hands, marveling at how smart my sisters must be to be able to read and write Chinese.

The aunties are all smiling at me, as though I had been a dying person who has now miraculously recovered. Auntie Ying is handing me another envelope. Inside is a check made out to June Woo for $1,200. I can't believe it.

"My sisters are sending *me* money?" I ask.

"No, no," says Auntie Lin with her mock exasperated voice. "Every year we save our mahjong winnings for big banquet at fancy restaurant. Most times your mother win, so most is her money. We add just a little, so you can go Hong Kong, take a train to Shanghai, see your sisters. Besides, we all getting too rich, too fat." She pats her stomach for proof.

"See my sisters," I say numbly. I am awed by this prospect, trying to imagine what I would see. And I am embarrassed by the end-of-the-year-banquet lie my aunties have told to mask their generosity. I am crying now, sobbing and laughing at the same time, seeing but not understanding this loyalty to my mother.

"You must see your sisters and tell them about your mother's death," says Auntie Ying. "But most important, you must tell them about her life. The mother they did not know, they must now know."

"See my sisters, tell them about my mother," I say, nodding. "What will I say? What can I tell them about my mother? I don't know anything. She was my mother."

The aunties are looking at me as if I had become crazy right before their eyes.

"Not know your own mother?" cries Auntie An-mei with disbelief. "How can you say? Your mother is in your bones!"

"Tell them stories of your family here. How she became success," offers Auntie Lin.

"Tell them stories she told you, lessons she taught, what you know about her mind that has become your mind," says Auntie Ying. "You mother very smart lady."

I hear more choruses of "Tell them, tell them" as each Auntie frantically tries to think what should be passed on.

"Her kindness."

"Her smartness."

"Her dutiful nature to family."

"Her hopes, things that matter to her."

"The excellent dishes she cooked."

"Imagine, a daughter not knowing her own mother!"

And then it occurs to me. They are frightened. In me, they see their own daughters, just as ignorant, just as unmindful of all the truths and hopes they have brought to America. They see daughters who grow impatient when their mothers talk in Chinese, who think they are stupid when they explain things in fractured English. They see that joy and luck do not mean the same to their daughters, that to these closed American-born minds "joy luck" is not a word, it does not exist. They see daughters who will bear grandchildren born without any connecting hope passed from generation to generation.

"I will tell them everything," I say simply, and the aunties look at me with doubtful faces.

"I will remember everything about her and tell them," I say more firmly. And gradually, one by one, they smile and pat my hand. They still look troubled, as if something were out of balance. But they also look hopeful that what I say will become true. What more can they ask? What more can I promise?

They go back to eating their soft boiled peanuts, saying stories among themselves. They are young girls again, dreaming of good times in the past and good times yet to come. A brother from Ningbo who makes his sister cry with joy when he returns nine thousand dollars plus interest. A youngest son whose stereo and TV repair business is so good he sends leftovers to China. A daughter whose babies are able to swim like fish in a fancy pool in Woodside. Such good stories. The best. They are the lucky ones.

And I am sitting at my mother's place at the mahjong table, on the East, where things begin.

FOR DISCUSSION

1. Why does Auntie An-mei tell Jing-mei that the mahjong club "got smart" and started investing in the stock market and playing mahjong for fun rather than money? How does this enable everyone to "have some joy"? (129)

2. Why do Auntie An-mei's Chinese relatives demand more money and gifts from her when she comes to visit them? Why does Jing-mei think of this story as "shameful"? (137)

3. Why do the women in the mahjong group give Jing-mei the money to go to China to meet her half sisters?

4. Why does Jing-mei promise them she will tell her half sisters "everything" about their mother after telling them she didn't really know her mother? (142)

FOR FURTHER REFLECTION

1. Is it better for immigrant groups to be assimilated or to retain their traditional culture?

2. Can you compete with someone else for money and remain good friends with them?

Katy Lederer (1972–) was born in Concord, New Hampshire. She was educated at the University of California, Berkeley and the Iowa Writers' Workshop, where she was an Iowa Arts Fellow. Lederer is the author of the poetry collections *Winter Sex* (2002) and *The Heaven-Sent Leaf* (2008). Her book *Poker Face: A Girlhood Among Gamblers* (2003) is a memoir about growing up as the younger sister of Howard Lederer and Annie Duke, game-playing East Coast intellectuals who became world-class poker players. She has won many fellowships and awards, including the Academy of American Poets Prize. From 1997 to 2007, Lederer edited the magazine *Explosive*. In addition to writing, teaching, and editing, she has also worked at a hedge fund in New York City. She encountered the phrase "the heaven-sent leaf," referring to paper money, in a translation of Goethe's *Faust*.

The Heaven-Sent Leaf

The speculation of contemporary life.
The teeming green of utterance.

To feel this clean,
This dream–éclat.

There is, in the heart, the hard-rendering profit.
As if we were plucking the leaves from the trees.

Let us think of the soft verdure of the spirit of this age as
    now inside of us and swollen by spring rain.
To imagine oneself as a river.

To imagine oneself as a stretch of cool water,
Pouring into a basin or brain.

And if one knows one is not free?
One crawls from the back of the head to the river

And places one's pinkie oh so cautiously in.

FOR DISCUSSION

1. What is meant by "the teeming green of utterance"? (145)

2. Why is profit described as "hard-rendering" and likened to "plucking the leaves from the trees"? (145)

3. Starting with the line that begins, "Let us think of the soft verdure," what is the poem suggesting that we do? (145) How are these suggestions related to the statements about life in the first six lines of the poem?

4. Why does the poem end with the image of someone crawling to the river and placing a "pinkie oh so cautiously in"? How is this action related to knowing "one is not free"? (145)

FOR FURTHER REFLECTION

1. What is Lederer suggesting in this poem about the relationship between money and the natural world?

2. What kinds of monetary transaction would you define as "speculation"? (145) Is it possible or desirable to avoid such speculation in the contemporary world?

Comparison Questions

1. How might Karl Marx respond to Henry David Thoreau's experiment of living at Walden Pond? How might Thoreau respond to Marx's ideas about money's effect on people?

2. Would Barbara Ehrenreich be more likely to see John Cheever's Johnny Hake as a victim of society or as a villain?

3. How might Harriet Jacobs react to Zora Neale Hurston's depiction of Joe and Missie May in "The Gilded Six-Bits"?

4. To what extent are the emotions and obligations of receiving money the same for Theodore Dreiser's Carrie and Amy Tan's Jing-mei? In what ways are their situations different?

5. Would Henry David Thoreau agree with the attitude toward money expressed in Katy Lederer's "The Heaven-Sent Leaf"?

6. What might Paco Underhill say about Carrie's and Drouet's trip to the department store and the purchase of Carrie's coat?

About Shared Inquiry

Shared Inquiry™ is the effort to achieve a more thorough understanding of a text by discussing questions, responses, and insights with fellow readers. Careful listening is essential. The leader guides the discussion by asking questions about specific ideas, problems of meaning, and passages in the text, but does not seek to impose a personal interpretation on the group.

During discussion, participants consider a number of different ideas and weigh the evidence for each. Introducing ideas and then refining or abandoning them are valuable parts of the interpretive process. Participants gain experience in communicating complex ideas and in supporting, testing, and expanding their thoughts. Everyone in the group contributes to the discussion. While participants may disagree with one another, they treat one another's ideas respectfully.

This process helps participants develop an understanding of important texts and ideas, rather than merely catalog knowledge about them. The following guidelines keep conversation focused on the text and assure that all participants have a voice:

1. **Read the selection carefully before participating in the discussion.** This ensures that all participants are equally prepared to talk about the text.

2. **Support your ideas with evidence from the text.** This keeps the discussion focused on understanding the selection and enables the group to weigh textual support for different interpretations.

3. **Discuss the ideas, themes, and formal elements in the selection and try to understand them fully before exploring issues that go beyond the selection itself.** Adequate reflection on the selection and various interpretations of it will make the exploration of broader issues more productive.

4. **Listen to other participants and respond to them directly.** Shared Inquiry is about the give-and-take of ideas, the willingness to listen to others and talk with them respectfully. Directing your comments and questions to other participants in the discussion, not always to the leader, will make the discussion livelier and more dynamic.

5. **Expect the leader to only ask questions.** Effective leaders help participants develop their own ideas, with everyone gaining a new understanding in the process. When participants hang back and wait for the leader to suggest answers, the discussion tends to falter.

Acknowledgments

All possible care has been taken to trace ownership and secure permission for each selection in this anthology. The Great Books Foundation wishes to thank the following authors, publishers, and representatives for permission to reprint copyrighted material:

The Gilded Six-Bits, from THE COMPLETE STORIES, by Zora Neale Hurston. Reprinted by permission of HarperCollins Publishers.

The Housebreaker of Shady Hill, from THE STORIES OF JOHN CHEEVER, by John Cheever. Copyright © 1978 by John Cheever. Reprinted by permission of Alfred A. Knopf, a division of Random House, Inc.

Selling in Minnesota, from NICKEL AND DIMED: ON (NOT) GETTING BY IN AMERICA, by Barbara Ehrenreich. Copyright © 2001 by Barbara Ehrenreich. Reprinted by permission of Henry Holt and Company, LLC.

Sex and the Mall, from CALL OF THE MALL, by Paco Underhill. Copyright © 2004 by Yobow, Inc. Reprinted by permission of Simon and Schuster, Inc.

The Joy Luck Club, from THE JOY LUCK CLUB, by Amy Tan. Copyright © 1989 by Amy Tan. Reprinted by permission of G. P. Putnam's Sons, a division of Penguin Group (USA) Inc.

The Heaven-Sent Leaf, from THE HEAVEN-SENT LEAF, by Katy Lederer. Copyright © 2008 by Katy Lederer. Reprinted by permission of BOA Editions, Ltd.